FINDING GOD in the Garden

FINDING GOD in the Garden

Devotions for Every Season

Editors of Guideposts

Finding God in the Garden

Published by Guideposts Books & Inspirational Media
100 Reserve Road, Suite E200, Danbury, CT 06810. Guideposts.org
Copyright © 2022 by Guideposts. All rights reserved.

This book, or parts thereof, may not be reproduced, stored in a retrieval system, or transmitted in any form or by any means, electronic, mechanical, photocopying, recording or otherwise, without the written permission of the publisher.

ACKNOWLEDGMENTS

Every attempt has been made to credit the sources of copyrighted material used in this book. If any such acknowledgment has been inadvertently omitted or miscredited, receipt of such information would be appreciated.

Scripture quotations marked (AMPC) are taken from the *Amplified Bible Classic Edition*. Copyright © by The Lockman Foundation, La Habra, California. All rights reserved.

Scripture quotations marked (CEB) are taken from the *Common English Bible*. Copyright © 2011 by Common English Bible.

Scripture quotations marked (CEV) are taken from *Holy Bible: Contemporary English Version*. Copyright © 1995 American Bible Society.

Scripture quotations marked (CSB) are taken from *The Christian Standard Bible*. Copyright © 2017 by Holman Bible Publishers. Used by permission.

Scripture quotations marked (ESV) are taken from the *Holy Bible, English Standard Version*. Copyright © 2001 by Crossway Bibles, a division of Good News Publishers. Used by permission. All rights reserved.

Scripture quotations marked (KJV) are taken from the *King James Version of the Bible*.

Scripture quotations marked (NASB and NASB1995) are taken from the *New American Standard Bible*. Copyright © 1960, 1962, 1963, 1968, 1971, 1972, 1973, 1975, 1977, 1995 by The Lockman Foundation, La Habra, California. Used by permission.

Scripture quotations marked (NCB) are taken from the New Catholic Bible. Copyright © by Catholic Book Publishing Corp., Totowa, NJ. All rights reserved.

Scripture quotations marked (NCV) are taken from *The Holy Bible, New Century Version*. Copyright © 2005 by Thomas Nelson.

Scripture quotations marked (NIV) are taken from *The Holy Bible, New International Version*. Copyright © 1973, 1978, 1984, 2011 by Biblica, Inc. Used by permission of Zondervan. All rights reserved worldwide. zondervan.com

Scripture quotations marked (NKJV) are taken from *The Holy Bible, New King James Version*. Copyright © 1982 by Thomas Nelson.

Scripture quotations marked (NLT) are taken from the *Holy Bible, New Living Translation*. Copyright © 1996, 2004, 2007 by Tyndale House Foundation. Used by permission of Tyndale House Publishers Inc., Carol Stream, Illinois. All rights reserved.

Scripture quotations marked (NRSV) are taken from the *New Revised Standard Version Bible*. Copyright © 1989 by the Division of Christian Education of the National Council of the Churches of Christ in the United States of America. Used by permission. All rights reserved.

Scripture quotations marked (RSV) are taken from the *Revised Standard Version of the Bible*. Copyright © 1946, 1952, 1971 by the Division of Christian Education of the National Council of the Churches of Christ in the United States of America. Used by permission.

Scripture quotations marked (TLB) are taken from *The Living Bible*. Copyright © 1971 by Tyndale House Publishers, Inc., Carol Stream, Illinois. All rights reserved.

Scripture quotations marked (TLV) are taken from *Tree of Life Version of the Bible*. Copyright © Messianic Jewish Family Bible Society. All rights reserved.

Cover design by Pam Walker, W Design Studio
Interior design by Pam Walker, W Design Studio
Cover illustration by Elena Medvedeva, Dreamstime.com
Typeset by Aptara, Inc.

978-1-961126-95-4 (hardcover)
978-1-961126-96-1 (softcover)
978-1-955877-88-6 (epub)

Printed and bound in the United States of America
10 9 8 7 6 5 4 3 2 1

When you accept the fact
that sometimes seasons are
dry and times are hard and that
God is in control of both, you will
discover a sense of divine refuge,
because the hope then is in
God and not in yourself.

CHARLES R. SWINDOLL

INTRODUCTION

"The glory of gardening: hands in the dirt, head in the sun, heart with nature. To nurture a garden is to feed not just the body, but the soul."

ALFRED AUSTIN

What makes gardening so pleasurable? What is it about this sometimes arduous activity that makes us want to do it again and again, season after season? Here are a few ideas.

The first is that gardening was humankind's very first occupation. After planting the Garden of Eden, God commissioned Adam "to work it and take care of it" (Genesis 2:15). This job gave Adam purpose, allowing him to find his place in creation and to share in the wondrous work of the Creator. Like Adam, many of us have inherited the desire to cultivate God's green earth and feel connected to nature when we dig, sow, and reap.

Second, gardening reflects life itself. Both gardening and life are impacted by the seasons—some when hard work yields a bountiful reward and others when it does not. Gardening ultimately teaches us patience and the power of hope. In the words of the poet May Sarton: "Everything that slows us down and forces patience, everything that sets us back into the slow circles of nature, is a help. Gardening is an instrument of *grace*."

Lastly, gardening delights our souls precisely because it is a spiritual activity as much as it is a practical task. In addition to requiring physical effort, gardening demands our complete trust. Even when we cannot see nature at work when we sow a tiny seed in the soil, we can be hopeful that someday—after taking the time to lovingly care for and nurture it—that very seed will flourish into a glorious plant, beautiful and strong.

Finding God in the Garden will take you on a journey as you dig, weed, sow, and reap, filling your soul with the assurance that—no matter the situation or season—God is always with you. Come alongside the writers as they share the parallels of their faith life with the elements of tending a garden, trusting that the seeds they plant in faith will blossom a hundredfold.

—EDITORS OF GUIDEPOSTS

I *wonder if the snow loves the trees and fields that it kisses them so gently? And then it covers them up snug, you know, with a white quilt; and perhaps it says, "Go to sleep, darlings, till the summer comes again."*

LEWIS CARROLL

Winter

My Life, God's Garden

CATHY BRYANT

I am the true vine, and My Father is the gardener.

JOHN 15:1 (TLV)

The Gardener wanders through the garden, His eyes taking in all the work to be done. Everywhere He looks, there are areas that need His attention. Weeds exist side-by-side with healthy plants, threatening to consume all the water and nourishment from the soil.

He stoops to look more closely at the dirt. Hard-packed, dry, and stony. More work.

The Gardener stands once more, yet this time His eyes don't register the work that must be done. Instead, He sees what can be. That sunny spot would be perfect for a flowering vine. And with a little soil improvement, most of the area would be more than capable of producing an abundant harvest of fruit and beauty.

Yes, this garden would take years of effort and work, but in the end, the results would be well-worth any expense of time and effort.

God is truly the Gardener of my soul and life. Sometimes when I look in the mirror and see myself as I am, it's enough to make my shoulders sag in defeat. How can I ever reach that place of getting past my human frailties to be the productive person God desires?

That's the good news in this story, in His story.

Because of Jesus, who is the Vine, God is able to take a life humbly submitted to His care and tending to produce in me far more than I could ever hope for or imagine.

Yes, it will take work. And sometimes that digging, pruning, and weeding can be painful. But if I'm willing to allow the Gardener to do His work in me, I will look back in gratitude for what He does in me and through me. God rejoices with me, quiets my heart, and brings me into a fuller life in Him.

Dear God, help me realize the spiritual lessons I can glean from the garden so that I may come to know Your generous love in a deeper way. Amen.

REFLECTIONS

Tree of Hope

KAREN SARGENT

At least there is hope for a tree: If it is cut down, it will sprout again.

JOB 14:7 (NIV)

A lush weeping willow tree overlooks the pond behind our house. Long, green fronds droop from the top to the ground below. Three winters after we planted it, an ice storm ravaged its tender branches. When spring arrived, no green appeared on them. By summer, we decided to cut down the tree. I was heartsick. Another winter came followed by a new spring. And there, next to the stump of the original tree, a new sprout appeared—flimsy and fragile but boasting green buds.

That sprout is now a strong, solid trunk that supports healthy, graceful branches. Every morning as I gaze through my kitchen window at the willow tree, I am reminded of its resilience. Against the odds, a single sprout was determined to rise up and thrive, and it did.

Father, when I feel defeated, You give me hope, like a damaged tree that sprouts again. Amen.

"MY FAITH IS LARGER THAN THE HILLS"

BY EMILY DICKINSON

My Faith is larger than the Hills—
So when the Hills decay—
My Faith must take the Purple Wheel
To show the Sun the way—

'Tis first He steps upon the Vane—
And then—upon the Hill—
And then abroad the World He go
To do His Golden Will—

And if His Yellow feet should miss—
The Bird would not arise—
The Flowers would slumber on their Stems—
No Bells have Paradise—

How dare I, therefore, stint a faith
On which so vast depends—
Lest Firmament should fail for me—
The Rivet in the Bands

Special Delivery

KATHRYN SLATTERY

The wilderness and the dry land shall be glad; the desert shall rejoice and blossom like the crocus; it shall blossom abundantly and rejoice with joy and singing.

ISAIAH 35:1–2 (ESV)

On a blustery December morning, I sat at the kitchen counter, placing a phone order for Christmas sweaters. As hold music played, I gazed out the window into our tiny backyard.

The paint on the white wooden gate was cracked and flaking. A bright red cardinal was perched on the edge of our old concrete birdbath, now filled with dead leaves and ice. I've always wanted a garden lush with flowers, birds, and butterflies. But all I had was that shoddy space.

The salesperson came back on the phone and asked if I had any instructions for the delivery person.

"Tell them it's easier to come around back," I said.

I hung up the phone and looked out the window again. *If only I had a bigger, prettier backyard*, I thought. *If only I had a garden.*

Three days later the front doorbell rang.

"Oh dear," I said, signing for the package. "I'm sorry you had to walk all the way around."

"No problem," the delivery man replied. "I started around back, but when I saw your garden, I didn't want to disturb it." He smiled and went on, "I love gardens, even in winter. Yours is so lovely. I can just picture how beautiful it is in the spring, with the flowers and birds at the birdbath."

I stared at the package in my hands, not knowing what to say. He thought our miniature backyard was a garden. A *lovely* garden.

"Thank you," I mumbled.

Suddenly, I could hardly wait for spring—to give the old gate a fresh coat of paint and to scrub the birdbath and fill it with cool, clear water. I imagined myself putting on my gloves, digging in the dirt, and planting geraniums, begonias, and petunias. I could practically smell the loamy earth and could almost feel the warmth of the sun on my back.

All I'd expected that day was a box of Christmas sweaters. But God had delivered so much more—the garden I'd always wanted. One that had been there all along.

Blooming in Winter

CANDEE FICK

And the God of all grace, who called you to his eternal glory in Christ, after you have suffered a little while, will himself restore you and make you strong, firm and steadfast.

1 PETER 5:10 (NIV)

At the end of every growing season, there comes a time of dormancy. The leaves turn colors and fall to the ground. We heap mulch over delicate roots to protect them from the coming cold. Fall turns into winter with shorter days, freezing temperatures, and piles of snow.

Yet, in the middle of these drab days, hope still blooms. Case in point? The Christmas cactus.

I have one of these unique plants. It was a gift from the members of a Bible study I led. The pot, wrapped in green foil, found a new home near my kitchen sink. Days after bringing it home, the lone bloom dropped. Christmas came and went without a glimpse of color. Well, that is, any color besides green.

I watered the cactus weekly. Green leaves sprouted new green leaves. I turned the pot, so the cactus got an even distribution of sunlight. And I wondered if it was worth the work. I mean, how many blooms would I get? One? Three? Five?

Winter faded into spring and outside my flowerbeds came alive with tulips and daffodils. Summer burst onto the scene with roses and strawberries. Months passed and the chrysanthemums added their color to the yard. Leaves changed colors and fell to the ground as fall gave way to snowstorms.

And, indoors, still sitting beside the sink, the cactus stayed green.

Then, months later on a snowy day, I caught a glimpse of a different color. A tiny bump of pink on the tip of a green leaf. On closer inspection, I found more of them. As the buds grew, so did my anticipation. Until one day, the buds opened. Large blooms of deep pink. A winter miracle.

My blooming cactus served as a timely reminder that hope still blooms in the middle of harsh or somber times. That spring will come again. It always does.

Every gardener knows that under the cloak of winter lies a miracle.

LUTHER BURBANK

The Flower of Hope

SUSANNA FOTH AUGHTMON

May the God of hope fill you with all joy and peace as you trust in him, so that you may overflow with hope by the power of the Holy Spirit.

ROMANS 15:13 (NIV)

My mom is an expert gardener. My dad, her right-hand man, accomplishes her botanical visions.

Last year they loaded a water-filled kiddie pool into the back of their rental car just so they could transport three hydrangea bushes. They drove over seven hundred miles to plant them in my front yard!

Hydrangeas, with their clustered blooms, are my favorite flower. But I panicked this winter when the blossoms shriveled on the stem.

I called my mom and she reassured me, "Don't worry," she said. "They'll come back."

She was right: they came back with a vengeance. Flower upon flower, full of life and hope.

God often allows new growth to flower in my life after a difficult season. He resurrects dreams, ushers in mercy, and breathes new life into desperate moments with His undeniable love.

Lady Bird Johnson said, "Where flowers bloom, so does hope." Yes! And the flower of hope is the most beautiful of all.

God, allow Your hope to flower in my heart, putting down deep roots, showing off Your beautiful love. Amen.

REFLECTIONS

A New Creation

MICHELLE COX

And I will give them one heart, and a new spirit I will put within them. I will remove the heart of stone from their flesh and give them a heart of flesh.

EZEKIEL 11:19 (ESV)

When I tire of winter, I glance longingly at gardening websites, dreaming of all the colorful spring and summer blooms that will someday brighten my days. I'm anxious for the soft green that will appear on the long branches of the weeping willows. I love watching them blow gracefully in the wind like a grandmother's shawl.

The other day, I made a couple of discoveries that gave me hope that spring truly is coming. The robins—God's first harbingers of spring—have started appearing in my yard again. And in the drab brown of my flowerbed, tender green shoots have begun to appear. I know from experience that in a few weeks, some new creations will grow there.

Tulips will bob their heads in the breeze, and jonquils will provide splashes of sunny yellow.

I'm grateful that God looks at the dormant places in my life and sees a new creation, sees what He desires to grow there.

I hope I bloom as beautifully for Him as my spring flowers do for me.

"O MASTER, LET ME WALK WITH THEE"

BY WASHINGTON GLADDEN

O Master, let me walk with thee
in lowly paths of service free;
tell me thy secret, help me bear
the strain of toil, the fret of care.

Help me the slow of heart to move
by some clear, winning word of love;
teach me the wayward feet to stay,
and guide them in the homeward way.

Teach me thy patience; still with thee
in closer, dearer company,
in work that keeps faith sweet and strong,
in trust that triumphs over wrong.

In hope that sends a shining ray
far down the future's broadening way,
in peace that only thou canst give,
with thee, O Master, let me live.

The Mystery of Life

GAIL THORELL SCHILLING

The seed sprouts and grows, though he does not know how.

MARK 4:27 (NIV)

Ever since I used my crayons to draw pictures of seeds in second grade, labelling them "sedes," I've been fascinated by them. I could never figure out how a tiny, dried-up brown speck might be buried in the dirt and then emerge green as a bean or a flower just about the time I had given up on it. Yet even as a child, I knew God had a hand in the process.

For years, with my own children, I shared the miracle of sprouting seeds on a wet paper towel in the garden and in pots on the windowsill. Later, my granddaughter Hannah was delighted when marigolds popped through soil in a paper cup and when an avocado pit, suspended in water, sent down roots and turned into a skinny tree.

Nowadays, my children and granddaughter continue gardening traditions on their own. So when I wintered in Florida and a nearby elementary school needed volunteers to teach students about seeds, I leapt at the chance. Still, I wondered whether kids raised on twenty-first-century technology would find the plants and my lessons at all interesting.

Clare, our leader, identified the sepals, petals, stamens, and pistil using a large model flower. The third graders identified the same parts on a real flower with petals, a freesia. Then, using a plastic knife, we carefully sliced open the bulbous ovary at the top of the stem and showed the students how to view the contents with a hand lens.

"Oh my!" blurted one little boy. "There's a seed in there!"

Oh my, indeed!

God, You amaze another generation with the mystery of life. Thank You for the seeds You plant in us. Amen.

REFLECTIONS

The Big Picture

CATHY BRYANT

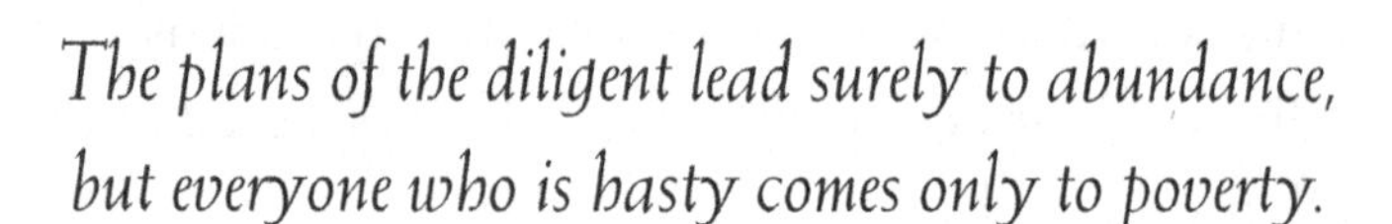

The plans of the diligent lead surely to abundance,
but everyone who is hasty comes only to poverty.

PROVERBS 21:5 (ESV)

In the winter, as I think ahead to what my summer garden will hold, there is much to consider. The best gardeners I know are discerning, diligent, and make a plan long before it's time to break ground. When the earth is covered in snow and ice and summer sun feels decades away, take time to plan your own garden.

Consider the soil you'll use. The best soil for plant growth is loam, often called topsoil or "black dirt." Loam is a mixture of sand (40 percent), clay (20 percent), and silt (40 percent). What makes loam so great for gardens is that while it retains water, it also drains well. It also holds onto nutrients but allows oxygen to permeate.

Consider your zone. If you are in the US, take a look at the USDA Plant Hardiness Zone Map to discern which plants will grow best where you are. There are 13 zones, and the lower numbers represent the colder climates. If you live in Zone 3, buying plants that thrive in Zone 9 would be a mistake; they couldn't stand the cold.

Consider the areas of sun and shade on your property and the needs of the particular plants you want to grow.

Some plants require full sun, while others cannot tolerate direct sunlight.

These elements, as well as the presence of water, the amount of space a plant needs, bloom times and lengths, and more will affect how well your garden grows, and all of these things *can* be planned for.

Similarly, we can take a good long look at our spiritual lives and what is ahead for us in the coming year. *What is the condition of our "soil"? What will water us? When should we lie fallow, and when should we plant?*

Ask the Master Gardener to lead you, give you fresh ideas, and accompany you as you grow with Him this year.

How many lessons of faith and beauty we should lose if there were no winter in our year!

THOMAS WENTWORTH HIGGINSON

The Brushing Technique

SABRA CIANCANELLI

Build houses and settle down; plant gardens and eat what they produce.

JEREMIAH 29:5 (NIV)

To get a head start on our garden, we sprout our tomatoes indoors from seeds. We plant them in a cute little germination station that we move around the house, from window to window, finding the best sunlight.

My favorite part of tending to the tomato plants—the part that touches my heart—happens when the glorious little green stems surface from the dirt. I give each seedling a soft touch, from left to right, up and down, a few times a day, to encourage strong stems. This is known by gardeners as "the brushing technique." By gently touching or brushing a folded piece of paper on seedlings, we recreate the effect of the blowing wind, making the plants stronger.

When I first learned about the brushing technique, I wondered if it was related to stress. Was a little pressure the same idea as that old maxim, "What doesn't kill you makes you stronger"? For a long time I believed that was the case, but this morning I changed my theory.

Today as my hands grazed each plant, I thought that maybe the brushing is more about caring enough to take a moment to reach out and be a part of its growth. Afterward, the herbal fragrance of the plants, the smell of spring, was left on my hands, reminding me of the beautiful exchange that happens when we care for another. The benefit of our effort changes and strengthens us as well.

Heavenly Father, thank You for the gift of caring, for the fulfillment I receive from planting seeds and watching them grow, and for creating fruit that nurtures my mind, body, and spirit. Amen.

~ Be Patient and Trust ~

A field of tulips is magnificent to see; it's as though the earth has been carpeted in vibrant hues. But what about a bucket of tulip bulbs? Seeing those feels decidedly less exciting. Are there parts of *your* life that feel less like a tulip field and more like a bunch of bulbs? Parts that have yet to germinate, sprout, and burst into color? Gertrude Jekyll was a British horticulturist who created over 400 gardens in the United Kingdom, Europe, and the United States in her lifetime. She said, "A garden is a grand teacher. It teaches patience and careful watchfulness; it teaches industry and thrift; above all it teaches entire trust."

Trust that, like a tulip bulb, God will make something beautiful out of your life.

Staking Trees

CATHY BRYANT

For the grace of God has appeared, bringing salvation to all men, instructing us to deny ungodliness and worldly desires and to live sensibly, righteously and godly in the present age.

TITUS 2:11–12 (NASB1995)

Of the thousands of plants I've grown in my lifetime, trees are my favorites. As described in the book of Genesis, they are pleasant to look at and good for food. And such variety! From the gracefulness of a weeping willow to the sturdy stalwart oak to delicious food-producing nut and fruit trees, these plants are amazing.

In Texas, the wind blows just about all the time, and staking new trees is very important. This staking helps the trees grow straight and true. Without it, they'd be bent permanently, leaning toward the north.

Like unstaked trees, many of us have a tendency to let the winds of life shape us. From life's problems to its temptations, it's no wonder that those not staked to God and His plans for their lives will grow crooked and bent out of shape, leaning whichever way the wind happens to blow that particular day.

In sharp contrast, those planted and staked to God grow straight and true, their life courses determined by the One who created them and loves them first and best. It is truly a blessed life that is staked to One who is true and straight and upright, even when the winds come.

Thank You, Lord, for all of Your blessings. In those times when my restless mind wanders to other things, quickly remind me of the importance of staying staked to You. Amen.

REFLECTIONS

Rejuvenation

SCOTT WALKER

For six years you shall prune your vineyard.

LEVITICUS 25:3 (ESV)

Although my wife, Beth, and I are not skilled gardeners, we enjoy nurturing potted plants. The column-lined porch of our old Southern house is draped with hanging ferns and filled with tropical hibiscus—these are my favorite plants, native to my childhood home in the lush Philippine Islands. Hibiscus grow to be large shrubs and produce red, orange, and yellow trumpet-shaped flowers. Framed by dark green leaves, the flowers make me smile each morning as I see the new life that has bloomed overnight.

As winter approaches, however, Beth prunes our hibiscus plants to a smaller size. I wince to see the branches shortened as we bring them into the warmth of our house. I do not like the pruning process. But my wife assures me it is the winter pruning that allows the plants to erupt into new and vital rejuvenation when spring arrives. In spring, the hibiscus will explode with growth, and flowers of astonishing beauty will reappear.

Pruning is necessary for plants' vitality. And so it is with my life. Sometimes I have to be cut down to size by a change in circumstance in order to be prodded into new growth and creative activity. It often comes with the change of seasons. I became a youth minister in my young adulthood, a pastor during middle age, and a professor in my senior years. Each development required a pruning process, and all led to new growth, new beauty, and new fruitfulness of labor and creativity.

Father, may I not dread Your pruning process, but instead may I trust You to help beauty and life to appear in me. Amen.

~ Recognize Your Uniqueness ~

Dreaming about next year's garden in winter, one person might envision a harvest of tomatoes, basil, and zucchini. Another might imagine a pollinator garden, butterflies flitting around pink milkweed and bees alighting on spikey purple coneflowers. Someone else might dream of a meditative rock garden with mosses, a fountain, and succulents. Like different types of gardens, the beauty you bring to the people around you and to your community is unique to you. Like a garden, it's born of God's vivid imagination.

Yielding to the Plan

CATHY BRYANT

But now in Christ Jesus you who once were far away have been brought near through the blood of Christ.

EPHESIANS 2:13 (NIV)

Making crop rotation part of a garden plan is wise. Different plants require varied levels and types of nutrients from the soil. Even after just one growing season, the soil can be depleted of the nutrients needed for a particular crop.

The sage gardener takes this into consideration and, over the years, moves crops to different locations to promote both healthy plants and an abundant harvest.

Additionally, there are plants that need to be transplanted for one reason or another. Perhaps the area has grown shady, and a particular plant needs abundant sunshine to produce. Or maybe a certain plant has outgrown the current location. If we don't transplant them to another area, their growth will be stunted.

There are many analogies here concerning my spiritual life. My Gardener always takes into consideration what I need at any particular moment in time. And sometimes what He *knows* I need and what I *think* I need don't match.

So, although I often don't understand why, He sometimes rotates me to a different location and sometimes plants me in a new kind of soil.

When His plan and my desires clash, I know it is best for me to yield to His plan rather than force my own. I need to keep in mind that, in His Sovereignty, God knows exactly what I need and is ever looking out for my health and growth. When I allow Him to do this work in my life, I can rest assured that I will become more like Him and produce an abundant crop for His Kingdom.

Father God, though I don't always like it, I appreciate Your leading and guiding my life. Thank You for transplanting me into Your Kingdom. Help me to fully grasp all that means for both my life and the lives of those I touch. Grant me the strength and ability to yield to Your perfect plan so that I may learn to produce much for You no matter where I am planted. In the name of Jesus—who was transplanted to this world for our sakes—I pray. Amen.

God's Imagination

ERIKA BENTSEN

Now faith is the substance of things hoped for,
the evidence of things not seen.

HEBREWS 11:1 (KJV)

On a late winter day, I went over to Mom's house and found her in the greenhouse. She was sitting in the sunlight among numerous pots of soil, the day after planting.

"What are you doing in here?" I asked. The thought of sitting around a bunch of barren flowerpots seemed depressing.

"Oh no, it's beautiful," she replied. "I'm imagining what they will be. You could say I'm dreaming in flowers."

Her words resounded in me.

I had been a cattle rancher, but a back injury put an end to my career. I shriveled up, mired in devastation, not sure who I was anymore, not sure what I should be doing with my life. How could I use my skills?

But God saw me as more than my profession and, over time, miraculously led me to a richer, fuller life. He imagined a better life for me, just as Mom imagined those seeds shooting up and blooming.

I'm still in the country surrounded by the animals I love. I've watched God throw open doors for me that I thought were closed when I was working on the ranch, like getting married to my best friend and devoting more time to my writing.

God filled my life after ranching with joy, not sorrow. When I put my trust in Him and began to follow His path, I actually viewed my grievous back injury as a *blessing*. Because of it, the Master Gardener has helped me grow beyond anything I could ever have dreamed of, and I know He isn't finished with me yet.

Dear Lord, please nurture me into becoming the flower You planted. I want to lift up my face to You and shine with all of the love You have given me. Amen.

REFLECTIONS

Hardening Off

CANDEE FICK

When Pharaoh let the people go, God did not lead them on the road through the Philistine country, though that was shorter. For God said, "If they face war, they might change their minds and return to Egypt." So God led the people around by the desert road toward the Red Sea.

EXODUS 13:17–18 (NIV)

Once you've got your seedlings started and the soil prepared, it's still not quite time to put the plants in the ground. Not only do you have to wait for the weather to warm up, but the baby plants need a period of hardening off before they can survive the harsh world.

Hardening off, as gardeners use the term, is a process of gradually exposing seedlings to sunlight, wind, and uneven temperatures. You see, young and fragile plants raised in the protected environment of a greenhouse can go into shock when exposed to the real world. They need to adapt and acclimate to their new surroundings through increasing periods of exposure to the outdoor conditions. This slow but sure process thickens the surface of the leaves and prevents excess loss of water later.

What's that got to do with my life?

Well, some of my dreams and ideas are fragile seedlings. If I were to launch them into the world prematurely, they might wither and die. A new piece of writing, for instance, might wilt away when exposed to the harsh red pen of an editor. So I expose my ego and writing gradually, slowly but surely. A writing group here. A critique partner there. I acclimate; my skin gets thicker, and I can withstand the winds of correction and critique.

When God delivered the Children of Israel out of slavery in Egypt, He hardened them off. That is, instead of leading them along the shortest path to the Promised Land, God led them the long way through the wilderness. Why? Because they would face war on the other path. And facing difficulties too soon might make them turn back instead of moving forward.

And God always wants us to move forward, and sometimes He needs us to harden off as we get started.

Forgives Neglect

SABRA CIANCANELLI

Blessed is the one whose transgressions are forgiven, whose sins are covered.

PSALM 32:1 (NIV)

"Forgives neglect" reads the description for sunflower seeds in my wildflower catalog. Looking over catalogs of seeds and bulbs is one of my favorite things to do. There's something peaceful and hopeful in looking forward to a field filled with blooms.

Growing up, I spent fall and winter evenings sitting on the couch next to my mother, her nose deep in a bulb catalog and a writing pad resting beside her so she could jot down her order. A single mother with four children, Mom always made time for a flower garden. And when the bulbs came in the mail, together we would push them into the earth.

"They'll be beautiful," Mom would say. "Just wait."

Months later, a cold winter behind us, the bulbs I had forgotten about would begin to sprout. I was too young to understand exactly why those spring blooms meant so much to my mother. She kept watch as the pale green shoots rose from the cold ground. Each bloom was too precious to cut.

Forgives neglect. I couldn't get past those words. Tiny seeds that would grow to the king of flowers, standing strong, heavy head filled with hundreds of small blooms that follow the sun—even if I neglected them.

I circled the sunflower seeds in the catalog and pictured exactly where they'd sprout and flourish in my backyard.

Lord, thank You for the sunflowers that remind me of Your boundless forgiveness. Amen.

~ Follow Instructions ~

Even experienced gardeners read the back of seed packets before planting. Concise, clear, and inspiring, these instructions tell us what to expect as our garden grows. These directions keep us from planting sun-loving flowers like zinnias in the shade.

Like words on a seed packet, God's commandments are similar; they inspire us and keep us growing healthy and strong.

Windows of Opportunity

CATHY BRYANT

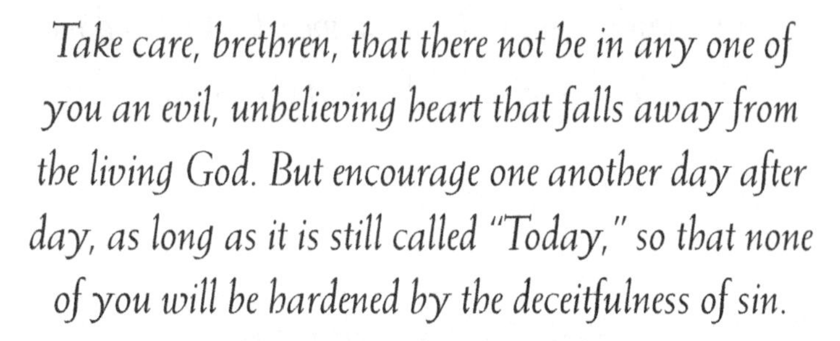

Take care, brethren, that there not be in any one of you an evil, unbelieving heart that falls away from the living God. But encourage one another day after day, as long as it is still called "Today," so that none of you will be hardened by the deceitfulness of sin.

HEBREWS 3:12–13 (NASB1995)

During the 365 days each year provides, we have a small window of opportunity for each part of the gardening process: planning, soil preparation, purchasing plants and seeds, growing seedlings, planting the garden, watering, weeding, pruning, and harvesting. If we miss even one of these windows of opportunity, it affects all of the subsequent parts of the process.

The same is true with our lives. We have a small window of opportunity to accept the work of Christ in our life's garden. The above passage from Hebrews calls it "today."

In all truth, none of us are guaranteed another breath or beat of our heart. So we would be wise to allow God entrance into our gardens to do His divine work without hardening our hearts toward Him through unbelief or wasting time.

I know I have only a small window of opportunity with each person I come in contact with throughout my days. Will I love them like Christ commanded me to do? Will I feed those who are hungry? Visit those who are lonely? Will I share God's love with them? I can, by recognizing the windows of opportunity God has placed in my life.

God, time can be a double-edged sword. On one hand, it is a gift from You, an opportunity to allow You access to my life and to share Your love with others. On the other hand, it is fleeting. Teach me to number my days, Lord, to make the most of every opportunity to love and serve You while it is still today. Amen.

REFLECTIONS

Mother's Orchid

CARLA HENDRICKS

Behold, I am doing a new thing; now it springs forth, do you not perceive it? I will make a way in the wilderness and rivers in the desert.

ISAIAH 43:19 (ESV)

Last summer, I bought my mother a beautiful orchid. My mother loved flowers and kept a charming home adorned with them. In the evenings, she'd sashay through the house, watering and spraying life into her precious "plant friends."

Two months after I'd given my mother the orchid, she had surgery. Her doctor placed a defibrillator near her heart, hoping to compensate for her weakened heart. I flew from Arkansas to Maryland to be with her and to assist Dad. When I arrived in their home, I was delighted to see the orchid healthier and donning even more blooms than it had during the summer.

At Christmastime, she was hospitalized again. I spent nearly two months watching her body become sicker and weaker. I also noticed that the orchid was also becoming sicker and weaker. It mirrored the life of its owner. Soon Mom succumbed to an infection and passed away in the new year. I had no hope that her sweet orchid would survive.

Two months after my mother passed, I returned to Maryland to help my sister pack up and prepare our parents' house to be put up for sale. I was amazed to see the orchid. It had sprung to life, gorgeous and lush with purple blooms.

Mom's orchid reminds me that life continues. Even in our hardest hours, God is always at work, growing and blooming and surprising us with unexpected joy.

The God who made us also can remake us.

WOODROW KROLL

Where Hope Grows

MARY LOU CARNEY

But hope that is seen is no hope at all.
Who hopes for what he already has?

ROMANS 8:24 (NIV)

Yesterday I planted an indoor paper-white narcissus garden. I'd never done this before, but my gardening guide assured me it was easy. I started with five bulbs, nut-brown spheres with lime green tufts. I found a glass bowl and filled it with clear marbles. Then I nested the bulbs, shoulder to shoulder, in their sparkling new bed. *Now for the water. . .*

The directions were very clear: The water must be below the bulbs; if it covers them, they'll rot. They "sniff" the water and grow their roots down to it. Without that effort, there will be no blooms.

Today, the project complete, I look past the bulb bowl to my real garden outside. The ground is frozen, covered with a dusting of snow. Stems and leaves are a sickly yellow. Branches are stark and bare. I'm not a big fan of winter, but I think it serves a purpose in my life. I read more. I try out recipes for hearty soups. I sit in my prayer chair a bit longer. And I *hope*.

Planting this winter garden has reminded me that good things are worth waiting for. Things like that first spring walk on the beach or running through the sprinkler with my grandkids. And, for now, things like the paper-whites soon to be blooming on my kitchen table.

Give me patience, Father, to wait for the blessings You're sending my way. Amen.

REFLECTIONS

Love in Bloom

RHODA BLECKER

His shoots spread over his garden.

JOB 8:16 (RSV)

It was a sad little bromeliad, almost hidden behind healthier, showier plants on display in the grocery store. The "60% off" sticker slapped on the front of its plastic pot showed plainly what store management thought of it. My husband Keith reached down and picked it up.

"You've got a beautiful bromeliad at home," I said. "What do you want that one for?"

"It's got potential," he said.

I shrugged. "At least it's cheap." Taking care of the plants in our house was Keith's hobby, not mine.

When we got home, he put it on the windowsill over our kitchen sink, next to the beautiful bromeliad he'd been nurturing for months. The new one looked sickly, leaves discolored and drooping, stalk dry and dull. He peeled off the discount sticker and tossed it in the trash. I shook my head and left the plant care to him.

I don't notice the plants as much as I might, usually only when Keith points out something to me. So I didn't really look at the bromeliads for more than a week. Then I was putting some dishes in the sink and happened to glance up at the windowsill. The bromeliads looked almost like twins—firm, plump, shiny leaves, and each plant with a brightly colored bloom.

"What in the world happened?" I asked.

Keith smiled at me. "It just needed a little love."

God, let everyone who needs a little love
find it and bloom. Amen.

Minds are like flowers; they open
only when the time is right.

STEPHEN RICHARDS

Sacred Gardens

CATHY BRYANT

And the LORD will continually guide you, and satisfy your desire in scorched places, and give strength to your bones; and you will be like a watered garden, and like a spring of water whose waters do not fail.

ISAIAH 58:11 (NASB1995)

Gardens are sacred places.

Had it not been for the Garden of Eden, we would never have known the type of intimate relationship with God that is available to each of us. It was in that first garden that God walked with human beings, His creation, in the cool of the day. It was also there that He sought them out after their fall and lovingly made the first sacrifice and shedding of blood to create clothing for them.

Christ's greatest struggle took place in the Garden of Gethsemane, a place of blood-sweating prayer and submission to God's plan. Had it not been for this garden, could Christ have endured the suffering of the cross to win the greatest victory ever recorded? Could He, fully God, and yet fully man, have completed the mission for which He came to earth?

In the garden that held the tomb of Jesus, the women and disciples were the first to witness the miraculous. Had it not been for this garden, the first witnesses would never have had the firsthand knowledge necessary to grow the church. Indeed, it is this garden where victory over sin and death was won, giving us the assurance of resurrection, both in this life and the life to come.

And, joy of all joys, time will end in a garden for those of us who believe and profess Him as our Lord and Savior. I know I will one day dwell in the place of God's throne, among trees whose leaves are for the healing of the nations. It will be a place whose river is life flowing forth from our heavenly Father. Paradise will be restored, and I will reign with Him forevermore, casting my crown at the feet of Him who alone is worthy.

REFLECTIONS

Nearer God's Heart

JENNIE IVEY

Now the Lord God had planted a garden in the east, in Eden; and there he put the man he had formed.

GENESIS 2:8 (NIV)

When I was a child, my great-great uncle Luther was already an old man. He didn't seem like it, though. He stood straight and tall and had hands that were square and strong and deeply tanned.

He lived in a brick house with a big rectangular backyard surrounded by a solid wooden fence. It was designed to keep the bunnies out, though more than a few managed to find their way in. "I don't really mind," Uncle Luther would say with a smile. "I've got lettuce and carrots enough to share." The middle of the yard was devoted to all kinds of vegetables—not just lettuce and carrots—that grew in long straight rows and were a joy to behold.

But those veggies couldn't hold a candle to Uncle Luther's flowers. From early spring to late fall, something was always in bloom. Daffodils and tulips and iris in spring. Daisies and zinnias and black-eyed Susans in summer. Mums and pansies and goldenrod in autumn. And in winter, the snow-covered garden lay dormant, waiting for spring's warmth to arrive so the seasonal show could begin all over again.

In the middle of Uncle Luther's yard was a metal sign staked in the ground at just the right height for me to read the words and memorize them. Here's what it said:

"The kiss of the sun for pardon; / The song of the birds for mirth. One is nearer God's heart in a garden / Than anywhere else on earth."

A half-century has passed since Uncle Luther went on to his heavenly reward. But I think of him every time I stroll through my own garden.

Remind us, Lord, that heaven is under our feet as well as over our heads.

REFLECTIONS

Renewing Earth and Heart

BOB HOSTETLER

Create in me a pure heart, O God,
and renew a steadfast spirit within me.

PSALM 51:10 (NIV)

I recently moved to the southern Nevada desert. Having never before lived in such a climate, I wasn't sure what to expect. And I've learned a lot. One of the things that has amazed me is the effect a tiny rainfall can have on the area. It's delightful to see a brown-and-gray, rocky expanse of landscape turn green overnight after a mere sprinkling of rain.

Seeing this, I remember a quote by novelist Pearl Buck, who said, "Inside myself is a place where I live all alone and that is where I renew my springs that never dry up."

I've known dry periods and desert stretches in my life, and, of course, I probably haven't seen the last of them.

I'm comforted, though, with the knowledge that even a snippet of a prayer like "renew a steadfast spirit within me" (Psalm 51:10) can quickly transform the desert of my heart, turning it into a garden of God's goodness and grace.

Restore us to Yourself, Lord. Amen.

"WINTER RAIN"

BY CHRISTINA ROSSETTI

Every valley drinks,
Every dell and hollow:
Where the kind rain sinks and sinks,
Green of Spring will follow.

Yet a lapse of weeks
Buds will burst their edges,
Strip their wool-coats, glue-coats, streaks,
In the woods and hedges;

But for fattening rain
We should have no flowers,
Never a bud or leaf again
But for soaking showers.

The Perfect Blend

CATHY BRYANT

There is an appointed time for everything. And there is a time for every event under heaven—a time to give birth and a time to die; a time to plant and a time to uproot what is planted.

ECCLESIASTES 3:1–2 (NASB1995)

Sand can be a wonderful addition to garden soil because it holds moisture. Too much sand, however, will result in unhealthy plants—spindly and unfruitful due to a lack of nutrients.

A little clay mixed in with the soil also can be a good thing, as clay absorbs moisture and releases it slowly. But too much clay can turn the soil rock-hard in a drought or high heat, squeezing the life from the plant's roots.

Regular dirt is the basic ingredient for any garden, but if all you have is unimproved dirt—without nutrients—your garden cannot reach its fullest potential.

Fertilizer is an important addition to any garden because of the nutrients it provides for the plants, but too much of it will produce an in-ground heat that will fry your plants to a crispy brown.

Even small rocks are desirable in certain places to allow excess water to drain away from a plant's roots. But, of course, if there are too many rocks the soil is unbalanced.

How fascinating to know that a balanced blend of sand, clay, dirt, fertilizer, and rocks is what helps a garden reach its perfect fruit-bearing potential.

It's the same in my life. There are many things in my life that are good and beneficial in and of themselves. If I allow one thing to take precedence over another, though, the soil of my life gets out of balance, causing a less-than-successful crop. It is through God's Word that I can learn to view the garden of my life as a delicate balance, knowing that there is a time and a place for everything.

God, grant me Your wisdom to see this truth and order my life by it. Amen.

Happiness is not a matter of intensity but of balance and order and rhythm and harmony.

THOMAS MERTON

Faith in Action

KERI WYATT KENT

"What shall we say the kingdom of God is like, or what parable shall we use to describe it? It is like a mustard seed, which is the smallest of all seeds on earth. Yet when planted, it grows and becomes the largest of all garden plants, with such big branches that the birds can perch in its shade."

MARK 4:30–32 (NIV)

Winter is prime planting time for poppies. Poppy seeds are tiny—you've seen them on bakery rolls. If I hadn't seen it happen every year, I'd find it hard to believe that by late June, those tiny seeds will become bright pink puffy flowers the size of my fist.

Planting poppies requires faith—you simply scatter the seeds on the soil. In some years, I've even put them right on top of the snow.

Jesus often used seeds as a picture of the kingdom of heaven. He was not talking about a someday, somewhere-else kingdom, but rather a present reality.

Even when it's still winter, I trust spring will come. And I trust God will take my tiny acts of faith and grows them into something beautiful.

"THE LITTLE GARDEN"

BY AMY LOWELL

A little garden on a bleak hillside
Where deep the heavy, dazzling mountain snow
Lies far into the spring. The sun's pale glow
Is scarcely able to melt patches wide
About the single rose bush. All denied
Of nature's tender ministries. But no,—
For wonder-working faith has made it blow
With flowers many hued and starry-eyed.
Here sleeps the sun long, idle summer hours;
Here butterflies and bees fare far to rove
Amid the crumpled leaves of poppy flowers;
Here four o'clocks, to the passionate night above
Fling whiffs of perfume, like pale incense showers.
A little garden, loved with a great love!

Storm Winds

CATHY BRYANT

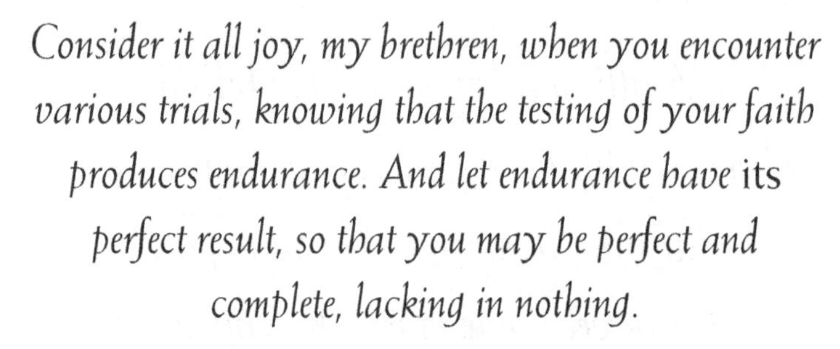

Consider it all joy, my brethren, when you encounter various trials, knowing that the testing of your faith produces endurance. And let endurance have its *perfect result, so that you may be perfect and complete, lacking in nothing.*

JAMES 1:2–4 (NASB1995)

The winds howled and lightning flashed as I stood at the window and peered out at the driving rain and the new fruit trees I had recently planted. The wind was so fierce that the baby trees bent low to the ground. Would they survive this late winter storm, or would I have to purchase and plant new trees?

Storms and rough weather in life happen to all of us. Sometimes storms catch us by surprise in their ferocity. And often dealing with the aftermath of the storm is more difficult than weathering the original storm itself.

The storm passed, and I continued to observe my saplings. The wind having died down, they stood up straight again. *They'll be fine*, I told myself. I've learned through my years as a gardener that experiencing winds and storms can actually *benefit* trees. Storms can strengthen them. You see, storm winds cause the outer layers of tree trunks to grow thicker in a shorter period of time. Winds also cause trees' root systems to grow deeper, supporting them as they grow taller.

Though it's much easier said than done, James 1:2 tells Christians to consider life's storms and winds "all joy." You see, it is during those times of struggle, and even suffering, that God can often do His best work in our lives, helping us grow deeper and more resilient.

REFLECTIONS

"THE SPARROW"

BY PAUL LAURENCE DUNBAR

A little bird, with plumage brown,
Beside my window flutters down,
A moment chirps its little strain,
Then taps upon my window-pane,
And chirps again, and hops along,
To call my notice to its song;
But I work on, nor heed its lay,
Till, in neglect, it flies away.

So birds of peace and hope and love
Come fluttering earthward from above,
To settle on life's window-sills,
And ease our load of earthly ills;
But we, in traffic's rush and din
Too deep engaged to let them in,
With deadened heart and sense plod on,
Nor know our loss till they are gone.

Tilling

CANDEE FICK

When a farmer plows for planting, does he plow continually? Does he keep on breaking up and barrowing the soil? When he has leveled the surface, does he not sow?

ISAIAH 28:24–25 (NIV)

While our seeds are sprouting indoors, it is time to prepare the soil outside—turn the ground over, stir organic material into the natural clay, loosen the dirt so plants have room to grow deep roots and air and water can circulate.

What about me? My life sometimes needs to undergo a period of upheaval too. I know if it doesn't then I risk becoming too hard, too set in my ways. Too rigid for new growth.

So how do I till my own life? I do it by embracing change. I create a new routine. Adopt a fresh outlook. Break an old habit. I shake things up, again and again, even if only for a season. I read a book by a new author. Take a different route home. Try a new recipe.

I don't embrace change alone, though. I look for God's guidance and ask Him to stay by my side as new growth emerges. By loosening the hard soil of my heart, I make room to sow the new crops God wants to plant. It is through Him that I will flourish.

Have No Fear

SABRA CIANCANELLI

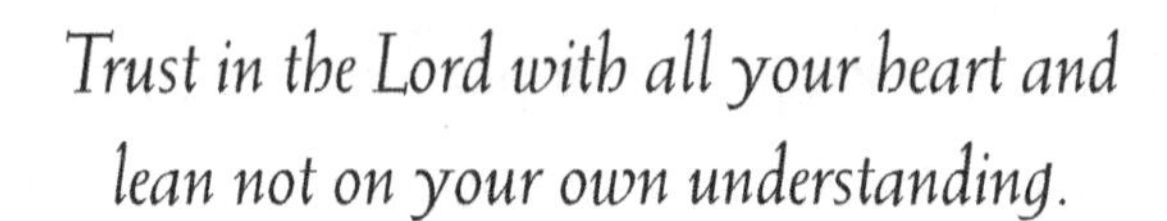

Trust in the Lord with all your heart and lean not on your own understanding.

PROVERBS 3:5 (NIV)

Bent over the soil, I cleared off leaves and began to wake up my garden, sweeping away winter's mess. My thoughts turned to an upcoming business trip. I had volunteered to go and was looking forward to it, but now, as the trip grew near, my excitement was turning to dread. Hands full of dead leaves, I found myself anxiously wondering: *Would the flight be delayed? Would my presentation go over well?* Just then, a garter snake slithered right in front of my knees! My heart jumped, and I let out a squeal.

Catching my breath, my mind traveled back to elementary school. In fourth grade, we had garter snakes in the classroom. On the first day of school, the teacher picked one up out of the tank and strolled the aisles between our desks. The snake slithered up his left arm, and we kids backed away, scooting our chairs.

"We're afraid of things we don't understand," our teacher said. "I'm going to teach you all about these amazing creatures. You don't have to touch them or go near them if you don't want to. But I'll bet by Thanksgiving each one of you will have held one. Anyone want to touch one now?"

I folded my arms and shook my head. I wasn't about to touch a snake, let alone hold one.

For a few minutes every morning, our teacher would go to the tank and pick one up. He showed us how snakes weren't slimy but strong. He offered facts and asked us to look closely, so we could see the beauty of their scales.

It didn't even take until Thanksgiving—before the end of September there wasn't one of us who hadn't grown to appreciate and care for these snakes. Not one of us feared them any longer. Settling back into my gardening tasks on that late winter day, I realized that I had nothing to fear: my business trip was going to be just fine.

Heavenly Father, help me to remember that
what is beyond my understanding is in Your hands.
I have nothing to fear. Amen.

The Little Things Make a Difference

MARION BOND WEST

Who dares despise the day of small things?

ZECHARIAH 4:10 (NIV)

I was in the doldrums. I'd stopped my regular walking and practically ceased cleaning the house. I couldn't bring myself to organize my office, the closet, or my messy dresser drawers. Even walking to the mailbox required a Herculean effort, which increased my depression.

When I was getting the mail one day, I noticed five tiny green shoots sprouting from the cement on top of our brick-encased mailbox. I lacked the energy to jerk them out. "You guys aren't going to make it," I said. "Nothing can grow in cement."

A few days later, two bright pink morning glories glared at me from the top of the mailbox. I guess the wind had blown seeds from our morning glories on the fence out back. Stunned, I began watering the foolish, brave little fellows. "I still don't think y'all can make it," I said, but I couldn't stop myself from smiling. Soon I began to admire the flowers, root for them, and finally even hope they'd flourish as I hurried each day to the mailbox.

Somehow during this strange saga, I managed to organize a terribly messy kitchen drawer. It was only one drawer, but I'd open it whenever I was in the kitchen just to revel in my accomplishment. Later, sitting on my closet floor, I straightened out the shoes I'd haphazardly tossed about for months. I even made a dent in the paper jungle in my office. And then—*tada!*—I put on my walking shoes early one fine morning and headed down the steep hill in front of our house. The resolute morning glories on the mailbox seemed to be cheering me on.

Father, please continue speaking to me through the little things all around me.

REFLECTIONS

Nothing Is Wasted

ANDREW SIEGEL

When they were filled, He said to His disciples, "Gather up the leftover fragments so that nothing will be lost."

JOHN 6:12 (NASB1995)

I made plenty of mistakes when I first took up gardening. Accidentally growing 25-pound Crimson Sweet watermelons instead of eight-pound Sugar Babies. Trimming back plants too quickly and too deeply to allow them to thrive. I still make mistakes, but I've discovered one of the most profound aspects of working in nature: *Mistakes are just opportunities in disguise*. Everything has a purpose, even if it's not the one I originally intended.

Take the spot I originally chose for my garden. It was way too shady for the plants to grow, but it turned out to be the perfect place for composting. I filled up the small square frame I'd planned on using for plants with vegetable and fruit peels, eggshells, and leaves. Now the things that most people toss in the trash provide nutrients for my plants. The compost pile is eventually consumed by worms and insects; then bacteria and microbes break it down into a rich soil I use to nourish the plants in our yard. Nothing is wasted.

I compost scraps and cardboard from our neighbors too. I use a barrel to conserve runoff water. Last year, I was able to donate 40 pounds of cucumbers to a food bank. Again, nothing is wasted.

As I wait for spring to arrive, I get ready by building garden beds using wood pallets thrown out by local grocery stores. I construct trellises from fallen branches of the oak in our backyard. And even if my homemade trellises don't work, they'll serve as lovely, original garden art.

In the end, it's not the lessons or even the produce that I've found the most valuable in my life as a gardener. It's the moments in the garden that make it my own little piece of heaven on earth. When my daughter, Penelope, brings me a worm she found while helping harvest tomatoes, or when we all dine on fresh vegetables from our backyard, I know we're growing much more than plants. We're growing a family and a sustainable way of life. And nothing is wasted.

Perhaps only when human effort had done its best and failed, would God's power alone be free to work.

CORRIE TEN BOOM

The Joy of Spring

EDIE MELSON

Peace I leave with you; my peace I give to you. Not as the world gives do I give to you. Let not your hearts be troubled, neither let them be afraid.

JOHN 14:27 (ESV)

I'm not much of a gardener. Although I love beautiful flowers, I don't have a good track record when it comes to making them grow.

During my son's first deployment to the Middle East, life conspired to change that. A few months after he left, a friend gave me a box of tulip bulbs. My face immediately betrayed my dismay, but she patiently walked me through the process of planting them. The bulbs would be put into the ground in the fall and would lie dormant all winter. They would then grow and bloom in the spring.

"When you see the leaves of the tiny flowers pushing toward the sun, you'll know it's almost time for him to come home," she said. "They'll give you hope when you need it most."

I thanked her, and then I left the carton in my garage, intending to ignore it. But every time I saw the box, its presence rebuked me. Finally, I gave in and ventured into my garden to plant them.

It was a long winter—cold and dark. I endured not only harsh weather but loneliness and fear. Dead leaves, frost, and finally a sprinkling of snow covered the area where I'd planted those bulbs. I soon forgot they were there.

Finally the weather began to turn, and one day, I saw that the tulips had begun to grow, their leaves forcing their way to the sun.

Day after day, it was as if those flowers were a physical representation of the hope I'd been afraid to let bloom during the winter months. Now with spring just around the corner and my son's homecoming in sight, nothing could keep either of us from straining toward the light.

Almost all of those bulbs bloomed, and each flower reminded me that I was one day closer to getting to hold my son in my arms again. I'll never forget what that long winter and those beautiful tulips taught me: God is always at work deep inside of me, bringing joy out in the open in His time.

And the Spring arose on the garden fair,
Like the Spirit of Love felt everywhere;
And each flower and herb on Earth's dark breast
Rose from the dreams of its wintry rest.

PERCY BYSSHE SHELLEY

Spring

The Best-Sown Seeds

JERRY MARTEN

Many are the plans in a man's heart, but it is the Lord's purpose that prevails.

PROVERBS 19:21 (NIV)

I was moving into a new house, and my greatest desire was to have an outstanding radish garden. I pored over gardening manuals until I knew exactly how to plant one, then I tilled the soil and buried the radish seeds precisely at the recommended depth. After completing the first row with perfectionist zeal, I stood back to study my handiwork. Suddenly a brown-and-white blur streaked by—our beagle puppy, Sam! He snatched the packet of radish seeds and tore off.

By the time I caught him, it was too late. The seeds were scattered haphazardly. My only consolation was that I had planted that one perfect row.

I had a small harvest of radishes that summer—only they weren't from my meticulously planted row. In fact, none of those radish seeds sprouted. Yet it seemed as if every single seed Sam had strewn in his pell-mell flight across the garden germinated and grew beautifully.

As I glanced between my barren row and the lush path sown by my puppy, I reflected that it is God, not I, who makes things grow. He is in charge.

"PUTTING IN THE SEED"

BY ROBERT FROST

You come to fetch me from my work to-night
When supper's on the table, and we'll see
If I can leave off burying the white
Soft petals fallen from the apple tree.
(Soft petals, yes, but not so barren quite,
Mingled with these, smooth bean and wrinkled pea;)
And go along with you ere you lose sight
Of what you came for and become like me,
Slave to a springtime passion for the earth.
How Love burns through the Putting in the Seed
On through the watching for that early birth
When, just as the soil tarnishes with weed,
The sturdy seedling with arched body comes
Shouldering its way and shedding the earth crumbs.

A Gratitude Share

SABRA CIANCANELLI

Ask the plants of the earth, and they will teach you.

JOB 12:8 (NRSV)

"Deep enough?" a little girl asked.

I nodded.

Carefully, she pushed cucumber seeds into the tiny hill of dirt we molded together and patted them down.

I was volunteering at the elementary school's garden project, a program where teachers bring their classes outdoors to learn about the earth. This group of kids was an inclusion class, meaning that some of them have special challenges.

One boy didn't seem to talk or make eye contact. He held tightly to his seeds and kept his focus on the dirt.

"Here, I'll show you," I said, crouching beside him and planting one.

Slowly, carefully, he positioned his five seeds into the soil.

Less than an hour earlier, I had been stressed about a writing deadline, but squatting in the dirt with all of these helping hands, my anxiety had vanished, replaced by the sun and the children's excitement.

When it was almost time for the group to leave, we sat in a circle in the grass. The teacher thanked everyone for helping and said, "Friends, let's have a gratitude share. If anything happened out here today that made you feel happy, you can share it with the group."

One girl raised her hand. "I'm happy for the garden because it's fun and I feel good. Oh, and I like to hear the birds sing."

Another child shared, "I'm grateful that we got to play in the dirt and see worms and bugs."

And then the boy who hadn't talked and was hesitant to plant his seeds raised his hand and in a loud, confident voice said, "I'm happy to grow stuff. I always wanted to grow something."

Dear Lord, thank You for today, for easing my anxieties and sowing seeds of Your glory that will take root and flourish in a child's heart. Amen.

I like gardening—it's a place where
I find myself when I need to lose myself.

ALICE SEBOLD

"SPRING"

BY GERARD MANLEY HOPKINS

Nothing is so beautiful as Spring—
When weeds, in wheels, shoot long and lovely and lush;
Thrush's eggs look little low heavens, and thrush
Through the echoing timber does so rinse and wring
The ear, it strikes like lightnings to hear him sing;
The glassy peartree leaves and blooms, they brush
The descending blue; that blue is all in a rush
With richness; the racing lambs too have fair their fling.

What is all this juice and all this joy?
A strain of the earth's sweet being in the beginning
In Eden garden.—Have, get, before it cloy,
Before it cloud, Christ, lord, and sour with sinning,
Innocent mind and Mayday in girl and boy,
Most, O maid's child, thy choice and worthy the winning.

A Seed Buffet

CYNTHIA RUCHTI

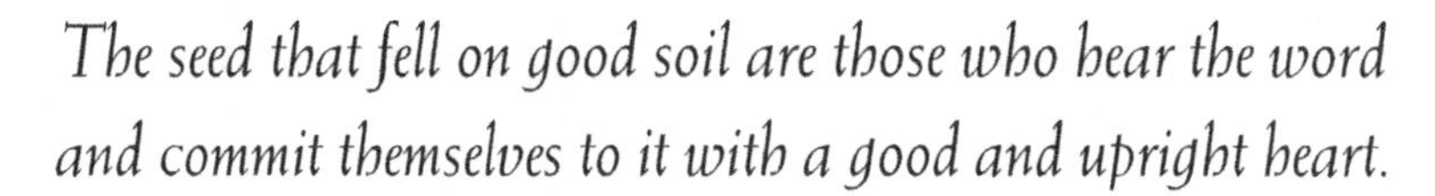

The seed that fell on good soil are those who hear the word and commit themselves to it with a good and upright heart.

LUKE 8:15 (CEB)

I'm a minimalist gardener. My husband built me raised beds so I don't have to bend over. I mulch with black fabric, so I don't have to weed. But I do appreciate the harvest.

The day I planted this year was perfect. Mixed days of warm sun followed by refreshing rain.

When I was cleaning up, I discovered a leftover hanging basket. I found an unused seed packet, planted the seeds, and hung the basket on the deck rail. The chipmunks found the basket just the right height for a seed buffet. And nothing sprouted. Ever.

Jesus told a parable that farmers and gardeners understand. It's about the sower, and I reflected on it when I saw my extra hanging basket. Those seeds were like the ones that fell on the path that birds snatched up. In my case, furry little striped "birds" feasted on them.

I love the end of that parable, about those who respond to Jesus's invitation to follow Him. We commit and through our resolve, we bear fruit.

The Pure in Heart

REBECCA BARLOW JORDAN

You are like whitewashed tombs, which look beautiful on the outside but on the inside are full of . . . everything unclean.

MATTHEW 23:27 (NIV)

Every spring, as soon as the frost is gone and daffodils appear, I'm ready to garden. A couple of years ago, however, I was determined to simplify the work but still make the garden as beautiful as possible. Perennials would return on their own, but I planned to cut back on annuals significantly. Replacing the struggling vegetable garden, my husband, Larry, and I planted low-maintenance and disease-resistant roses.

Even simplified gardening required dozens of hours of effort. We needed mulch and a lot of it—seventy-seven bags, to be exact! Weeding the beds and spreading mulch stretched into two months' worth of work.

When we finished, the gardens were indeed beautiful. Inside the house, the dust had gotten a little thicker, the bathrooms a little dirtier, and there were more smudges on the floor. I had been so focused on the *outside* of my house that I had neglected what was *inside*.

I read Matthew 23 recently. In it, Jesus used a white-washed tomb, a cup, and a dish to illustrate the legalism and hypocrisy of religious leaders He encountered. Evidently they worked hard at obeying rules—cleanliness and beauty on the *outside*—while neglecting their hearts.

Reflecting on my own experience, along with Jesus's powerful words, was a sober and helpful reminder: Jesus is most concerned with the beauty, cleanliness, and purity of what is inside my heart.

REFLECTIONS

A Gardening Lesson from God

DIANA AYDIN

Every branch in me that does not bear fruit he takes away, and every branch that does bear fruit he prunes, that it may bear more fruit.

JOHN 15:2 (ESV)

It was "New York Cares Day," where some 4,000 New Yorkers volunteered to help revitalize schools across the city. My sister's company formed a volunteer team, and I tagged along with them. We were tasked with sprucing up the gardens outside an elementary school on the Upper West Side.

One of the gardens was a tangle of weeds, with deep, almost woody roots. I grabbed a rake and tried loosening them. It was hard work! The roots were deep, and I knew I didn't have the stamina to keep digging away at these for the next several hours.

When our leader said there was another task to be done, I jumped at the chance to change jobs and paint the school's fence. The next few hours passed by quickly, and soon it was time to clean up for the day.

Turning around from the fence, I saw that garden where my day had begun. I barely recognized it.

"Oh my goodness!" I said. "This looks amazing!"

"Those roots were brutal. They had spread out over the entire space," one of the volunteers said. "We had to rip it all out."

A city garden gets a fresh start. The weeds had been replaced with fresh soil and plants. It was still a work in progress, but by the next spring, it would be a lovely spot for teachers and students.

Just then, I heard a message from God, loud and clear. He told me that all of us are like that garden. Our wounds and hurts are deeply rooted. They're tangled, and they keep us from being able to grow in the beautiful way He intends. God is at work in us, pulling and weeding. It's hard work, but He never gives up!

The result of His loving care? A garden transformed, brimming with life and possibility.

A Turkish Lent

GAIL THORELL SCHILLING

Evening, and morning, and at noon, will I pray.

PSALM 55:17 (KJV)

Morning in Istanbul had dawned flamingo pink and gold. When the *muezzin*, the person who proclaims the Muslim call to prayer, broadcast his message to the faithful every day, I felt inspired to use the reminder to pray as well. Sure, I still said my morning prayers and grace at meals, even alone during this retreat, but a few more prayers throughout the day seemed a worthy Lenten practice. Alas, my good intentions lasted only a few days before I lapsed into my irregular rhythm of prayer.

Some weeks later, I craned over my balcony to glimpse the Sea of Marmara, barely visible as blue haze to the east. Below, an elderly gentleman wearing a woolen skullcap carried a blue plastic tarp and rake across the lush lawn. I surmised he was a gardener for the apartment complex, as primroses bloomed in profusion; and tulips, a colorful symbol of Istanbul, poked a few inches through the warming earth.

While I was absorbed in this tranquil scene, the call to prayer rolled fuguelike from all the mosques in the city. The gardener began to pray right there on the lawn. He stood with his back toward me, facing east, palms outstretched. His blue tarp had become a prayer rug. He kneeled on it, prostrated himself, rose, and repeated the sequence several times.

The gardener literally dropped what he was doing to pray, and his devotion humbled me.

Minutes later, the gardener resumed his duties. I watched him rake under another bush, mound the debris onto his tarp, and disappear around the building.

Without a word, this stranger had forced me to rethink my own slipshod prayer practices and had modeled to me what faithfulness means.

REFLECTIONS

Spiritual Compost

JON SWEENEY

The Lord will send a blessing on your barns and on everything you put your hand to. The Lord your God will bless you in the land he is giving you.

DEUTERONOMY 28:8 (NIV)

My wife and I bought a ton (yes, two thousand pounds!) of compost for our Vermont garden one year. A backhoe slowly made its way down our street. When it arrived at our driveway, our neighbor slammed the gearshift into park, keeping the backhoe's engine rumbling, and called out, "Where should I dump it?"

"That corner over there," I told him, pointing past the end of the driveway. "Next to the garden."

It took us days to spread all of that compost. In the late-day sunshine, when we were done, you could actually feel the heat of the soil radiating.

Our garden was ready for planting, and in went the rows of beans, cucumbers, beets, carrots, broccoli, and lettuces.

Psalm 36:7–8 (NRSV) reads, "All people may . . . feast on the abundance of your house, and you give them drink from the river of your delights." I love these words. What revelry that is from the psalmist to God and as a promise to us.

The soil in our garden is like my soul, waiting for God. The compost is like all of the spiritual activities I fill my life with: prayer, Bible reading, spiritual conversations with friends, helping my neighbors.

Compost seasons the soil as prayer seasons the soul. And that backhoe? I imagine it is the church, particularly right now, when the services, traditions, and people who make it up all come together to deliver what I need the most.

Abundant Gardener, show me today where I may cultivate deeper soil and well-watered roots to You. Amen.

~ Let the Past Become Compost ~

Some gardeners call compost "black gold." With time, refuse like food scraps, eggshells, and grass clippings are transformed, and dead, discarded things turn into rich fertilizer. In what ways might the "compost" of your life nurture a future harvest, a new cycle of growth? Another truth about compost is that you can't rush its transformation; you just need to give it time, trusting that nature is working its miracle.

Trust God that He is turning the refuse of your life into something that gives new life.

Promised Beauty

SHARON HINCK

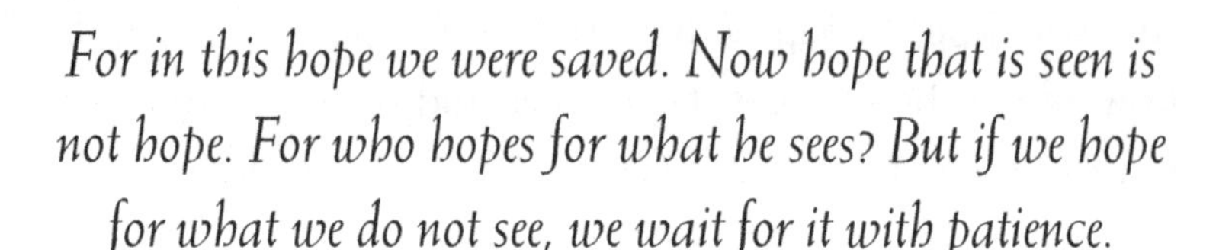

For in this hope we were saved. Now hope that is seen is not hope. For who hopes for what he sees? But if we hope for what we do not see, we wait for it with patience.

ROMANS 8:24–25 (ESV)

On a lovely spring day, my husband and I stopped at the park and found volunteers hosting a plant sale. Unlike at a garden center, there weren't photos accompanying the seedlings to show what they'd look like later in the season. Most had only a Popsicle stick saying "blue" or "lavender" or "yellow." I love blue irises, so we searched for those. We purchased them without seeing proof of what they would look like in bloom. At home, we planted the rhizomes in our garden with the trust that next year beautiful iris blossoms would grow.

Jesus has promised us many things. He promises He is with us to the ends of earth. But we can't see His presence. He promises us a home in heaven, but we have no realtor listing with a photo of what that will look like. He promises our sins are forgiven, yet we continue to fall short.

Like a young plant, we are not yet fully all we're intended to be.

We plant bulbs and rhizomes that look nothing like the blooms we long for. Yet we trust that, in time, the promised beauty will appear. If we can have faith that a gnarled root will produce flowers in the spring, we can also hope in the true and trusted promises of Jesus.

REFLECTIONS

A Poet and Her Jalapeño Plant

MARI PACK

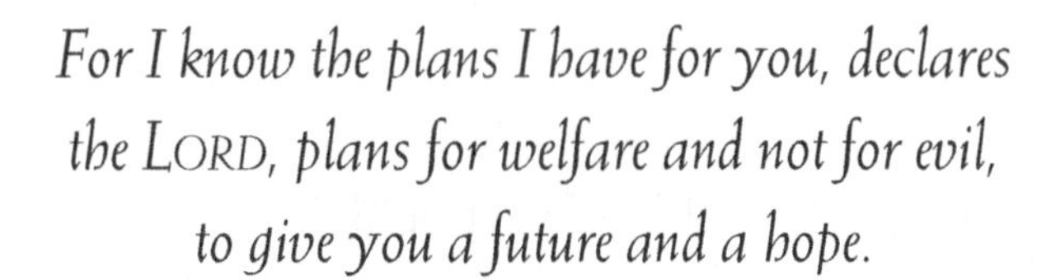

For I know the plans I have for you, declares the LORD, plans for welfare and not for evil, to give you a future and a hope.

JEREMIAH 29:11 (ESV)

After finishing the first year of grad school, a poetry MFA program, I was exhausted and riddled with self-doubt. When a professor asked about my plans, I blurted out a response.

"I'll be gardening!"

"Good idea!" he said. "Emily Dickinson loved gardening."

Emily Dickinson had lived on a homestead in Massachusetts and studied botany. I lived in a New York City apartment and had no gardening experience.

A few days later, I spotted seedlings for sale. Kale, herbs, and . . . a jalapeño plant. On a whim, I bought the jalapeño.

I called an urban farmer friend for advice. He told me that they need a lot of water and sunlight. He grew his outdoors in giant plastic tubs and said I shouldn't be surprised if my plant never bore fruit.

"Jalapeños *aren't* houseplants," he said.

I watered and changed the dirt for my little plant. I even talked to it. And, over the summer, it grew—a bit.

I started the second year of my program, but by December, my jalapeño was wilted and many of its leaves had fallen off. Still, I did my best to care for it.

Spring came, and my plant came back to life. It grew bigger, with new leaves. When I submitted my graduate thesis, a book of poems, it was flowering.

I was washing dishes one day when my professor called.

"Your poems are strong," he said. "Well done!"

Relieved and happy, I went back to the sink, but then noticed that the flowers on my plant were gone. I peered closer. Where a flower had been, a tiny green fruit pushed through, barely the size of a dime.

My jalapeño plant had grown right beside me. Both of us had done what I hadn't thought possible.

"Thank You, God," I whispered.

REFLECTIONS

Spring Cleaning

CANDEE FICK

For, before the harvest, when the blossom is gone and the flower becomes a ripening grape, he will cut off the shoots with pruning knives, and cut down and take away the spreading branches.

ISAIAH 18:5 (NIV)

The calendar said that spring officially started a couple of weeks ago, but we happened to be blessed with snow just three days later. That's Colorado weather for you. At least this time, the snowdrifts melted within days instead of weeks.

Once I could finally see my poor flower beds again, I was more than ready for spring to really arrive. Warmer weather stirred my anticipation, but there was a little something I needed to take care of first, something I didn't quite get to last fall when I should have.

I hadn't cleaned out the dead growth and matted leaves in my flower bed in the autumn, but it could wait no longer. It was time. Time to prune the rosebushes. Time to pick the windblown litter off the thorns and out of the rocks. All to make room for new growth to happen and to allow air and water and sun to reach the plants.

It was time for a little spring cleaning, both in my garden beds and in other areas of my life. I'm making room for new growth and opportunities by cutting out blocks of wasted time. I'm digging out old roots of bitterness and unforgiveness. Throwing away feelings of rejection and inadequacy. Dusting off neglected ideas.

Spring is coming to my heart, and I want to be ready to see what God has in store.

Feel God's presence within you, lifting you up,
and filling your heart with the deep abiding
assurance that all is well.

NORMAN VINCENT PEALE

Seed Viability

CATHY BRYANT

But Christ has indeed been raised from the dead, the firstfruits of those who have fallen asleep.

1 CORINTHIANS 15:20 (NIV)

Is there anything worse than working a particular patch of soil and planting seeds only to have *nothing* come up? There's a certain hope, expectation, and anticipation that goes along with planting. So when that hope, expectation, and anticipation aren't met, we feel—understandably—very disappointed.

Thankfully, in the spiritual realm we don't have to worry about that. The first book of John lets us know that Jesus is the Word of God—*He* is the seed. After His crucifixion, Jesus wasn't buried as much as He was *planted*. And three days later He sprung forth, victorious over death. And because of that, we know that death cannot defeat us.

You see, when the Apostle Paul wrote that Jesus was the "firstfruits" in the resurrection, he meant that He was the first "crop" of the dead to be resurrected. In Jewish culture, the "firstfruits" were the first of the season's harvest and they were offered to God. Firstfruits implies that there will be more resurrection fruit, and we believers are that fruit.

All of this is to say that this earth is not our final home. Instead hope, expectation, and anticipation of being resurrected like Christ awaits us. And with Jesus as the Word and the seed, we never have to worry about that seed not being viable.

Oh, Lord, how grateful we are for Jesus. Because of His resurrection, we will also be raised. That resurrection life has already burst into bloom in our hearts and lives. God, we're also grateful for the promise that wherever we plant the seed of Your Word, there will indeed be a crop that springs forth for Your Kingdom. May we be ever grateful for the opportunity to be workers in Your field. Give us boldness, fearlessness, and clarity of speech to better serve You. Amen.

REFLECTIONS

"SPRING STORM"

BY WILLIAM CARLOS WILLIAMS

The sky has given over
its bitterness.
Out of the dark change
all day long
rain falls and falls
as if it would never end.
Still the snow keeps
its hold on the ground.
But water, water
from a thousand runnels!
It collects swiftly,
dappled with black
cuts a way for itself
through green ice in the gutters.
Drop after drop it falls
from the withered grass-stems
of the overhanging embankment.

Growing Gratefulness

ASHLEY KAPPEL

Every good gift and every perfect gift is from above, coming down from the Father of lights with whom there is no variation or shadow due to change.

JAMES 1:17 (ESV)

At the first sign of spring, I gathered the kids and headed out to the country to pick flowers.

As we drove, I overheard the kids wishing they could have flowers in their rooms. My mom had always kept a small basket of flowers in my room, a few buds for me to nurture and observe. It taught me how to take care of something as well as what it felt like to be needed.

That afternoon, we planted tiny buds in three red pots and talked about how God blessed us with such beauty so we would find joy in Him.

Each morning, after that, my kids would come down the stairs, bubbling over about their plants—which ones had bloomed, which needed more sunlight or water.

Just as the plants growing outdoors made me feel rooted me in gratefulness and thanksgiving to my God, the blooms in their rooms reminded them of their Maker—and the wonderful things He was doing for them.

In the Details

TERRY CLIFTON

He will wipe every tear from their eyes. There will be no more death or mourning or crying or pain, for the old order of things has passed away.

REVELATION 21:4 (NIV)

I had received a diagnosis of terminal cancer. Feeling overwhelmed by all the instructions and advice from medical professionals, I found myself wondering, *Was the devil in the details? Where, then, was Jesus?* I sought the Lord.

As I drew close to Him in prayer, I felt Him draw close to me. In His presence, I knew that He had never abandoned me. He had been—and would ever be—with me.

I felt Jesus encouraging me to savor every moment with my precious wife. I heard Him telling me to cherish the afternoons I spent in the garden, working among the beautiful flowers and the happy moments each day when I played with our lovable cats. All of these things were gifts to me.

Jesus reminded me of yet one more gift—the gift of eternal life.

A year later, I was notified by doctors that my cancer was gone. But Jesus was not: He was still with me. The Lord, not the devil, was in the details of my life for now and eternity.

"PIED BEAUTY"

BY GERARD MANLEY HOPKINS

Glory be to God for dappled things—
For skies of couple-colour as a brinded cow;
For rose-moles all in stipple upon trout that swim;
Fresh-firecoal chestnut-falls; finches' wings;
Landscape plotted and pieced—fold, fallow, and plough;
And all trades, their gear and tackle and trim.

All things counter, original, spare, strange;
Whatever is fickle, freckled (who knows how?)
With swift, slow; sweet, sour; adazzle, dim;
He fathers-forth whose beauty is past change:
Praise Him.

God's Good Seed

CAROL MACKEY

Others fell on good ground and yielded a crop.

MATTHEW 13:8 (NKJV)

I grew up in inner-city New York where the only greenery around was the shrubs and patchy grass surrounding our public housing project.

After I got married, my husband and I bought a house in the suburbs with a small backyard. It was a dream fulfilled for me.

I'm a nature lover, and I've always admired houses accented with beautiful gardens and foliage. When we moved, I decided to try my hand at gardening. I'd never done it before and was a little nervous. I bought the prettiest blooms and a pair of gloves, and I got to work.

A few weeks later, I noticed one area of my garden was burgeoning, bursting with color, but the other was not. This was certainly not due to lack of care; I watered both sets of plants and added fertilizer to each, yet one set of plants looked neglected. What was I doing wrong?

I called in an expert.

"Your soil is no good over here," the landscaper said, after examining my garden patches. He pushed the toe of his shoe into the grainy dirt where nothing was in bloom.

I had planted good flowers in bad soil.

Jesus's parable of the sower immediately came to mind: The same seed placed in different environments will yield vastly different results. If the environment is not right, there will be no growth. Nothing will bloom and thrive. What began as a practical lesson in gardening morphed into a spiritual lesson.

As I read and study God's Word, the seed of faith He placed in me continues to grow and blossom. However, when I allow my heart to harden or if I plant myself in bad soil, there is no spiritual growth. I must keep the soil of my heart soft and become a receiver of "good seed"—God's Word.

REFLECTIONS

When to Send the Rain

PATTY KIRK

Ah Lord God! It is you who have made the heavens and the earth by your great power and by your outstretched arm! Nothing is too hard for you.

JEREMIAH 32:17 (ESV)

Workshops are held in the seminar room of the college where I teach: a long narrow space with a table just big enough for twelve and a large window on one end. We were about midway through a fiction workshop one day when the sun-filled view out of the window changed to a wall of rain.

"Oh no!" my students wailed, even as my heart filled with gratitude.

I pictured my little spring garden beds—the lettuces, spinach, and watercress that had looked so yellow and puny this morning all drenched in the downpour, now green and happy.

"How can you hate rain?" I asked my students.

They listed their answers: cancelled plans, getting drenched, awkward umbrellas, messed up hair! We are, of course, all different. We have different lives, desires, and needs. We have different things to grieve, different things to be grateful for.

I remember worrying, as a newcomer to my faith, about other believers' prayers and my own. What if they competed? For instance, what if I prayed for the miraculous healing of a friend's terminal disease and someone else prayed for her peaceful death? How can God answer both of us? That was my first faith struggle.

After a lifetime of miracles, however, I've come to worship a bigger God: the Doer of impossible feats. I rejoice as blithely as a child in my own momentary abundance—rain, health, the resolution of some current worry—and I leave the divvying up to God. In God's wisdom, He knows when to send the rain.

God, I believe in Your incredible power to respond in love to all of Your children. Thank You! Amen.

I love spring anywhere, but if I could choose, I would always greet it in a garden.

RUTH STOUT

Greening Up

CANDEE FICK

Forget the former things; do not dwell on the past. See, I am doing a new thing! Now it springs up; do you not perceive it? I am making a way in the wilderness and streams in the wasteland.

ISAIAH 43:18–19 (NIV)

As I cleaned out the flower beds, I discovered something growing under all the dead stuff. My hyacinth bulbs were peeking through the dirt. Had I not cleared out the damp, matted leaves, I would have missed them.

I moved on to the row of rosebushes and spotted that surprise of color again. At the base of each bush, green was creeping upward. It was as if the plant was slowly waking up.

Everywhere I turned, even more plants were greening. From the dry brown lawn to the tiny buds swelling on the tree branches, new life was emerging after the cold, dark winter.

What about in my heart? Could I see evidence of new growth in my life? Season after season in my spiritual journey, as I clear out what's holding me back and take care of my soul, I start to see life springing up in once-barren places.

Both in my garden and in my heart, winter may have been long and cold, but God always brings the spring.

"SPRING POOLS"

BY ROBERT FROST

These pools that, though in forests, still reflect
The total sky almost without defect,
And like the flowers beside them, chill and shiver,
Will like the flowers beside them soon be gone,
And yet not out by any brook or river,
But up by roots to bring dark foliage on.
The trees that have it in their pent-up buds
To darken nature and be summer woods—
Let them think twice before they use their powers
To blot out and drink up and sweep away
These flowery waters and these watery flowers
From snow that melted only yesterday.

Time to Call the Master Gardener

EDIE MELSON

Restore to me the joy of your salvation,
and uphold me with a willing spirit.

PSALM 51:12 (ESV)

I do not have a green thumb. Houseplants quiver in fear when I pass them at the garden center, knowing that a trip home with me means certain death.

But last year, I took a long look at our front yard. It wasn't a pretty sight. The once-neat flower beds were overgrown with straggling azaleas, weeds, and overgrown roses that no longer bloomed. These areas had once been well-defined by an edging of monkey grass, but even that had dead spots and areas of overgrowth that spilled into the yard.

It was time for some work.

I called in an expert. The landscaper came and mapped out a plan. He took inventory and assessed what would have to go and what could be trimmed and transplanted.

Over the next few weeks, he and his crew pulled off a major overhaul. First they removed everything and brought in new soil. The old soil had become depleted. Next he severely pruned the bushes and removed all the weeds.

At this point, the yard looked desolate, with ugly patches of dirt where flowerbeds used to be.

Sure enough, new topsoil, plants, and mulch were added. The beds were redefined and carefully edged with boundaries that would stay in place.

As I watched this process, I was struck by how similar this was to my spiritual life. Caught up in the busyness and stress of life, I'd let things get out of hand, and my life resembled a wilderness much more than a garden.

I took my troubles to the Master Gardener. He stepped in and, without judgment or condemnation, mapped out a plan. He did some painful pruning and got rid of the weeds that had choked my once-green relationship with Him. He added a layer of topsoil through His Holy Word to nourish my struggling faith. Finally He redefined boundaries I'd let collapse.

Our Father is faithful, and only He can cultivate anew the garden of our souls.

Planted Among Weeds

CATHY BRYANT

The Lord is not slow about His promise, as some count slowness, but is patient toward you, not wishing for any to perish but for all to come to repentance.

2 PETER 3:9 (NASB1995)

One thing I've learned in my years of gardening is that sometimes it's difficult to distinguish between the plants I've planted and impostors. Often, by the time I recognize a plant as a weed, it is impossible to remove it without damaging the plant I intentionally started from seed or seedling.

Similarly, in the mountains where we live, many varieties of mushrooms grow, including those that are edible. Unfortunately, for each type of edible mushroom, there is usually a deadly look-alike. Only those highly trained in the field of mycology are able to distinguish between the two.

Wheat is an amazing grain and has been described as the perfect food. I've even read articles that say wheat found inside the pyramids of ancient Egypt was still viable after thousands of years. But wheat has a look-alike, too, called darnel. At the early stages, darnel looks exactly like wheat, but it is a poisonous plant. In small quantities, it causes hallucinations. In large doses, it's deadly. Only through the maturation process can the difference between the two be seen. As the two ripen side by side, the wheat turns golden, while darnel turns almost black.

Isn't that a perfect description of those among us who have the appearance of godliness at the beginning, but as they ripen, show their true colors? Isn't it so often true that only as we mature are we able to discern between what is true and what is inauthentic?

The truth we can cling to is that God knows those who are His. God knows our hearts, our true intentions, thoughts, and deeds. Though He is patient, He also loves the truth. For those who have sought after and followed Him, He will gather us to our heavenly home where no weeds or lies or poison can harm us.

Jesus answered, "I am the way and the truth and the life. No one comes to the Father except through me."

JOHN 14:6 (NIV)

The Celebration of Spring

CANDEE FICK

See! The winter is past; the rains are over and gone. Flowers appear on the earth; the season of singing has come, the cooing of doves is heard in our land. The fig tree forms its early fruit; the blossoming vines spread their fragrance.

SONG OF SONGS 2:11–13 (NIV)

Something amazing happens in the spring. Grass turns green. Trees bud, readying themselves for new leaves. The bulbs I buried deep in the dirt last fall send up green leaves, their stalks stretching for the sky. Atop each, a bud forms and grows until it shows a hint of the color within.

Seemingly overnight, the flowers in my yard unfurl their petals in an explosion of color and fragrance. Hyacinths and daffodils. Tulips and lilies. The lilac bush and cherry blossoms follow. And then come the roses, the glorious roses.

It's a celebration long in the making.

My life is not so different from the blooming garden. I'm a wife, mother, legal researcher, Bible study leader, singer, friend, and writer. Each area is quietly growing behind the scenes and underground. And then, just at the right time, green shoots reach heavenward and buds form. My life blossoms in ways I could only have imagined during the bleak days of winter when things felt stalled or even frozen.

You see, while I might be in the winter season as a writer—slowly pounding out and polishing my work in private—hints of spring are emerging. They include positive comments from critique partners. Queries and proposals in the mail. Articles and manuscripts under consideration. Invitations to judge contests. Mentoring other writers. Slowly the buds of hope grow.

Spring is coming, and someday my personal garden will flower anew.

~ Embrace the Unexpected ~

"Volunteer plants" unexpectedly appear in the garden and require no effort on the part of the gardener. They weren't planted, but they have germinated from seeds dropped by birds or stuck to the fur of animals or after they've been blown there by the wind.

What or who are the volunteer plants in your life? Friendships that began in a serendipitous way? Opportunities that bloomed, seemingly out of nowhere? Ideas that took you by surprise?

Thank God for those blessings.

Mom's Rosebushes

LINDA KASSNER

For everyone who has been born of God overcomes the world. And this is the victory that has overcome the world—our faith.

1 JOHN 5:4 (ESV)

Mom was an excellent gardener, and everything she touched thrived. The rosebushes in her front yard with their huge, fragrant blooms were the envy of the neighborhood.

On the other hand, my sister, Mary Beth, and I didn't know the first thing about gardening. But early one spring morning, we stood in our mother's front yard with shovels and pruning shears, preparing to move Mom's beloved roses. Mom had passed away a few months earlier, and we were getting her house ready for sale. We wanted to transplant Mom's roses to our homes as a memorial to her.

"How do we move these roses without killing them?" Mary Beth asked.

"I have no idea," I said. "Mom would tell us exactly how to do this." I felt her loss more deeply than ever.

All at once, we were startled by a voice behind us.

"Are you digging up those beautiful rosebushes?" I turned and saw a young man holding a shovel.

"Yes," I said. "Well, trying to." We explained why we were there.

"I'll tell you just what to do," the man said. "Prune them back a little bit, then preserve as much of the root system as possible."

He described how to dig them up, how to fertilize the soil, the proper watering schedule once we planted them at our homes, and more.

"How do you know all of this?" my sister asked.

"I was once a gardener at the Denver Botanical Gardens," he said.

The man answered a few more questions, and I thanked him. I was just about to do what he had suggested when I realized I'd forgotten to ask his name, in case we needed more help. I stood and looked up and down the street. He was gone. Vanished. It couldn't have been more than a few seconds.

This gardener was surely an angel. And because of his heaven-sent advice, Mom's beautiful roses have bloomed in our yards ever since.

FROM

HOLY SONNETS

BY JOHN DONNE

Batter my heart, three-person'd God, for you
As yet but knock, breathe, shine, and seek to mend;
That I may rise and stand, o'erthrow me, and bend
Your force to break, blow, burn, and make me new.
I, like an usurp'd town to another due,
Labor to admit you, but oh, to no end;
Reason, your viceroy in me, me should defend,
But is captiv'd, and proves weak or untrue.
Yet dearly I love you, and would be lov'd fain,
But am betroth'd unto your enemy;
Divorce me, untie or break that knot again,
Take me to you, imprison me, for I,
Except you enthrall me, never shall be free,
Nor ever chaste, except you ravish me.

Remove It All

BY BOB HOSTETLER

I will give you a new heart and put a new spirit in you; I will remove from you your heart of stone and give you a heart of flesh.

EZEKIEL 36:26 (NIV)

One spring, my preteen daughter and I wanted to plant a vegetable garden. We mapped it out in our yard and started work. Soon we hit an obstacle: a large, heavy rock. We could've planted around it or moved the location of the garden, but we eventually removed the rock. That summer we enjoyed the fruits—and vegetables—of our labor, especially zucchini. Lots of zucchini.

It can be as hard—harder, even—to remove from my life the things that trip me up and tear me down. Some are external; many originate in me. Some are easy to remove; others are excavated only with great difficulty, even pain. So, I pray: "Remove." Remove it all. Remove it completely.

Lord, remove everything in my life that trips me up or tears me down. Amen.

A Garden that Brought Peace

CHUCK WEST

May your unfailing love be my comfort, according to your promise to your servant.

PSALM 119:76 (NIV)

The day my son Danny was murdered, he was hanging out in a motel with a few fellow drug users who decided to rob him. They hit his head too hard; he died.

It was April, when the sun shines and the air is fresh in Atlanta. Just a day earlier, my wife and I had bought spring plants, including a Japanese maple sapling.

Some days after Danny's funeral, I stood before the condolence gifts, bunches of plants in pretty pots. Staring at them, a thought began forming: *What if, instead of throwing these plants away, I put them in the ground? What if I created a memory garden? Might we find peace?*

Hacking into Georgia's hard clay dirt, I found myself railing with nearly every swing of the shovel. I cursed the drugs, the murderers. I called out to Danny: *Why? Why? Why?*

As the garden progressed, my anger started to subside. I arranged azaleas into eye-catching patterns of white, coral, and red. I bought a bench and situated it beneath a canopy of dogwood branches.

When I was done, I stood back and examined my handiwork. It looked good, but it lacked one thing: a focal point. I looked around the patio and saw that new maple sapling, still sitting in its pot. It was perfect, and I planted it. A few months later, the garden thrived—all except the Japanese maple, the tree I'd hoped would be the centerpiece of my garden.

Time passed, as it does. The following spring, the azaleas bloomed again. Everything was bright with new growth. I glanced toward the maple, about 50 feet away, and saw a patch of red in it. *Is there a cardinal in that dead tree?* I wondered. I walked outside to get a better look.

A small batch of red leaves was growing from a branch, shivering in the afternoon breeze. I reached out and touched one. It was soft and delicate. *Impossible,* I thought. *This tree had been dead, but now there was new life.*

I felt something move in me, something that felt like peace.

A Time for Planting

CANDEE FICK

Now the parable is this: The seed is the word of God.

LUKE 8:11 (ESV)

Now that my flower beds are ready, my fingers are itching for the garden. But I live in Colorado and it's too early to plant anything outside. It's actually *way* too early since it's been known to snow here even as late as mid-May.

Does that mean I'm out of luck as a gardener? No! There's plenty to do right now.

First, I plan. How big will the garden be? What varieties of vegetables and how many of each? Next, I get seeds. Planning to plant doesn't mean a thing unless I have the raw materials on hand when the day arrives. Last, I start seedlings, keeping them safely inside.

I remember trips to my grandparents' house and seeing my grandfather's greenhouse with rows of milk cartons, each with a tiny green shoot poking up through the dirt. A promise of things to come.

Just like my spring garden preparation, I need to identify what crop I want to grow in my life. *Love? Joy? Patience? Compassion? Friendships? Spiritual growth?*

Just like I can't get corn from a tomato seed, I can't grow compassion on a root of jealousy. I can't plant hours of television time and expect my work to get done. I can't expect my faith to grow without planting time in the Word and in prayer.

And I need to get started. Even if the weather isn't quite right outside for my tiny seedling to survive, I can still begin within a sheltered environment and, later when it's time, I can bring my growing seedlings out into the open air.

As for growing my faith and spending time with the Word, it's time to get started with that too.

Don't judge each day by the harvest you reap,
but by the seeds you plant.

ROBERT LOUIS STEVENSON

A Fierce Love

HEIDI GAUL

For I am convinced that neither death nor life, neither angels nor demons, neither the present nor the future, nor any powers, neither height nor depth, nor anything else in all creation, will be able to separate us from the love of God that is in Christ Jesus our Lord.

ROMANS 8:38–39 (NIV)

We keep several birdhouses in our yard. You can spy one in every corner of my garden, nestled among the branches or hanging from a shepherd's hook. Large, small, and everything in between—they bring whimsy and joy to the outdoor space.

Two of the tiny homes are occupied almost every year. My favorite hangs just above the hose bib. Every time I turn on the water to sprinkle the garden, I try to sneak a peek inside.

Before the eggs are laid, even as the male and female gather material for their nest, the flying parents-to-be perform a gallant show of courage. They dive-bomb me as I water the plants near their future babies' abode. These little creatures, not yet born, are loved with a fierceness so rare most of us can only imagine it.

Because I know Jesus, I'm blessed to understand that depth of this caring, the protective devotion He has for all believers. Nothing can separate me from His love. As I live each day, I'm secure in the knowledge that He is constantly watching over me, fighting on my behalf whenever necessary. He's dedicated to growing my faith to full maturity. He feeds me all I need in order to become a sound reflection of Him in the world.

Jesus's nurturing gives me wings to fly.

REFLECTIONS

Planning and Plotting

ANDREW SIEGEL

Commit your work to the Lord, and
your plans will be established.

PROVERBS 16:3 (ESV)

After successfully growing a hardy tomato plant, which began its life as a tiny shoot in a humble paper cup, I started thinking about what else I could grow. That year, my wife, Kathy, and I signed up for a class at a nearby nursery. At the end of the session, they gave participants some garlic bulbs to plant at home.

I wanted to use the garlic to start a real garden, but I quickly discovered my personality traits were the opposite of what a gardener needs. I was impulsive and scattered. I didn't think about where I placed the garden. I was not a planner!

The first spot I chose for our garden didn't get enough sunlight, and my seedlings struggled. After a few weeks, I replanted the garden in a sunnier location. Once again, things went awry. I hadn't anticipated how large the various plants would get, and I had planted them too close together. Next thing I knew, broccoli leaves were shading other seedlings and the corn had eclipsed the spinach that was growing in its shadow.

My garden needed the right amount of water and sun, good soil, and the proper spacing of plants. All of these were vital to a healthy garden. I realized I needed to make a plan.

I started filling a green spiral notebook with my sketches, plans, and ideas. I tracked the way the sun fell on our property. I measured the space and plotted out which plants could fit in the 40 square feet I had in my garden. By carefully planning ahead, I saved time and energy later—and my garden thrived.

I took that lesson into other areas of my life: my faith, my career, my parenting, and more. By planning ahead and taking note of what I and others need to thrive, I can help to create an environment that fulfills God's purpose.

Make sure you pay attention to what's right with your life, not just what's wrong.

NORMAN VINCENT PEALE

The Gift of Water

CANDEE FICK

He will descend like rain on the meadow,
like showers that water the earth.

PSALM 72:6 (NCB)

April showers bring May flowers. Or so my teachers would always say back in elementary school.

In order to grow a successful garden, you need nutrient-rich soil and a sunny spot—and water, of course! And not just water on the surface of the land, but deep down where the roots will eventually spread out. Whether it comes as a sprinkling or a downpour, consistent watering is necessary. And rain is a gift!

But when the rain comes, too often we complain about it. It ruins our picnic plans or forces the game to be canceled. It's all about perspective, though. Do we huddle under umbrellas or joyfully splash in the puddles? Do we find the sound of rain on the rooftop soothing or irritating? Do we remember that the rain is God's gift to the earth?

Like those April showers bringing May flowers, stormy seasons in life also help us to grow. But, when they come, do we let the refreshing moisture soak into our souls? Or does it run off the hardened clay of our hearts? Do I resent the cloudy days or learn to be thankful in the middle of storms?

God, keep my vision clear and let me know that when You send storms, they are filling up my own reservoir of strength so that I may grow. I thank You for the gift of rain! Amen.

Keep Watered

Different plants need different amounts of water. Plants with shallower root systems—including those grown in containers—need more water than those deeply rooted in the earth. Plants growing in hotter, dryer conditions need more water than those in moderate climates—in some cases, they need to be watered a few times every day.

What "waters" you? Time outdoors? Laughing with friends? Reading? Spending time in prayer? When you are feeling "parched," remember to keep yourself watered, like a healthy garden.

The Spirit's Fruit in Our Lives

CATHY BRYANT

Since we live by the Spirit, let us keep in step with the Spirit.

GALATIANS 5:25 (NIV)

One of my favorite harbingers of spring is the blossoming of the fruit trees. Not only does the blossom-laden air smell fresh and sweet, but each of those blossoms carries with it the potential for an abundant fruit harvest.

But difficulties soon arrive. As those hundreds of blossoms morph into tiny fruits, the responsibility of deciding what goes and what stays descends.

As a gardener, I hate thinning out the fruit. In fact, the first few times I dealt with taking care of fruit trees, I opted to leave all the fruit, greedy for *all* of it to do well. The fallacy of my greed soon became evident. Because there were so many pieces of fruit vying for the same tree to provide nourishment, none of them did well. The harvest resulted in small, undeveloped fruit that really wasn't good for anything. In addition, some of the branches grew so heavy from the weight of the fruit that they broke off before the fruit was ripe.

The analogy for my life is evident. I face those moments where I must decide what goes and what stays. I'd be wise to get rid of any bad fruit in my life in order to let the good fruit develop.

When I do this, I am, in effect, allowing God to reign in my life. If I stay in step with God's Spirit as the Gardener of my soul—if I allow Him to lead and guide me where He wants me rather than going my own way—the harvest produced will be large fruit, well-developed and useful. And the fruit of God's Spirit—His love, joy, peace, forbearance, kindness, goodness, faithfulness, gentleness, and self-control—will be mine as well.

God, keep me in step with Your Spirit and Your plan for my life. I am incapable of producing any fruit in my life apart from You, so lead me in the way that will be most productive for my life and for Your Kingdom. Amen.

Consider the Lilies

GAIL THORELL SCHILLING

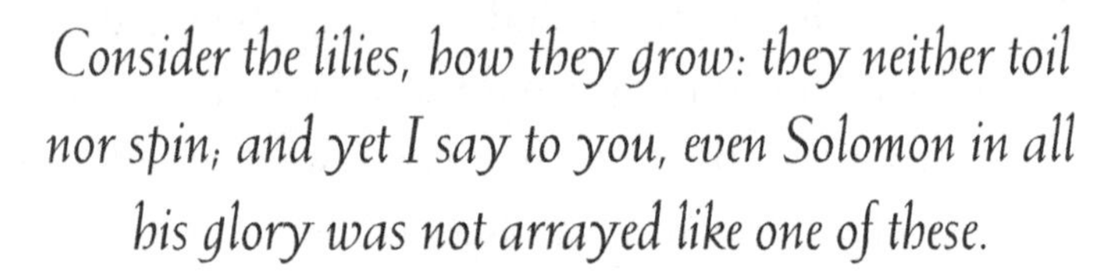

Consider the lilies, how they grow: they neither toil nor spin; and yet I say to you, even Solomon in all his glory was not arrayed like one of these.

LUKE 12:27 (NKJV)

As I gaze at a close-up photo of a daylily that my father grew, with raindrops beaded like quicksilver atop the ruffled petals, I'm reminded of the exuberant orange sunset over the Gulf of Mexico sunset. This photo is all I have left to remember Dad's lush gardens now. He died seventeen years ago, and both his home and the gardens he lovingly landscaped have been sold.

Daylilies like these often grow wild in New Hampshire. Many once grew alongside old cabins and farmhouses that have succumbed to fire or collapsed over the centuries. Deep in the woods, it's not unusual to find lilies blooming around the stone foundations and cellar holes, overgrown with weeds. How little they need in order to thrive!

So here in my new apartment, I consider the lilies and the rest of Jesus's teaching: Take no thought for your life. I believe this.

During my past four years of house-sitting, traveling, and writing, I found that I needed very little to thrive. God took care of my needs so that I could continue my creative work. Now, as I rebuild a more settled life in a home of my own, I marvel how once again God has uniquely provided for my needs through my friends. I see the lamp my friend Kathy gave me, the sofa from Ruth, drapes from Diana. And that's just the living room.

The photograph of my father's daylily will always be a part of my home, wherever I live. It reminds me of my father's love, as well as of the love of my heavenly Father. He always provides for me.

REFLECTIONS

Worth the Wait

ANDREW SIEGEL

Therefore, as God's chosen people, holy and dearly loved, clothe yourselves with compassion, kindness, humility, gentleness and patience.

COLOSSIANS 3:12 (NIV)

My wife, Kathy, and I had been married only a year when the medical equipment company I was working for shut its doors. It was devastating!

That had been my first real job, and losing it meant starting over. I applied for other jobs immediately, filling out applications until it felt like my eyes were glazed over. It seemed like I was sending them into a black hole: I received not a single response after submitting dozens of applications.

One day, I couldn't bring myself to fill out yet another job application. I headed to the kitchen for a snack. And, sitting on the counter, I saw the "grow your own tomato" cup Kathy had brought home from her job at a preschool.

I picked it up and popped off the plastic dome. I drizzled in a little water, like the instructions said, put the dome back, and set the cup on the windowsill. I didn't know anything about tomatoes, but I figured they probably needed light.

Over the next few days, I checked the plant obsessively, wondering if it would ever sprout. But then, the following week, a tiny green shoot appeared. *The plant was growing!* I transferred it to a larger cup and then, a few weeks later, into a coffee can. The plant just kept on growing. Soon it was four feet tall, living in a five-gallon pot on our back patio.

Patience, the plant seemed to be reminding me. *These things take time.*

Didn't that go for my job search as well? I diligently applied for more positions, reminding myself to be patient. Just like the tomato plant, I needed time to grow. A few months later, I got a job with a medical supply company, and the lesson has stayed with me.

The best things take time and care, and are worth waiting for.

REFLECTIONS

Bursting into Bloom

ASHLEY KAPPEL

It will burst into bloom; it will rejoice greatly and shout for joy.

ISAIAH 35:2 (NIV)

I do not have a green thumb and have managed to kill even the hardiest of herbs. So it should come as no surprise that my simple wish would be met with anxiety.

"I want to plant tulips," I told my husband, Brian.

"Sounds like a plan," Brian said, looking doubtful, if supportive.

I picked out bulbs, and then I read gardening blogs for step-by-step tips. I even filled my planters halfway with foam in order to make them lighter.

The first rain came, and I noticed the dirt rising in my planters. *That's interesting*, I thought. *The foam must be absorbing the water and swelling*. The next rain came and the dirt rose even higher, leading Brian to realize I'd missed one important pointer: cut holes in the planter to allow the rainwater to drain out. He helped me return the bulbs, now strewn across our deck, back into the planters.

When Brian's dad came to visit and inquired about the planters, I told him we'd encountered some trouble.

"Oh, let me guess," he said. "Did you plant the bulbs upside down?"

My face fell; now I quite possibly had waterlogged buds growing down into our pots instead of up.

Spring came quickly and tips of green began to poke through the soil. A few weeks later, the planters overflowed with bursts of color. In spite of my gardening shortcomings, there was beauty. I reflected on the truth that in my planters, as is the case in my life, God can turn mistakes and false starts into something truly beautiful.

Mistakes are the portals of discovery.

JAMES JOYCE

Summer set lip to earth's bosom bare,
And left the flushed print in a poppy there:
Like a yawn of fire from the grass it came,
And the fanning wind puffed it to flapping flame...

FRANCIS THOMPSON

Summer

An Urban Garden

REBECCA MAKER

Live in harmony with one another.

ROMANS 12:16 (NIV)

The heat was rising in waves from the concrete late one afternoon. I dodged tourists gaping at the Empire State Building and joined the throng of fellow commuters racing to the subway. Dashing down the stairs to the platform, I made it onto my train just before the doors closed.

Thirty minutes later I was in my Brooklyn neighborhood and headed for our raised beds in the community garden. I grabbed some green beans and cherry tomatoes for a salad, admired another gardener's sweet peas, and tugged off a basil leaf, breathing in the heady scent.

I hardly knew what a community garden was when I first read the notice about this one shortly after we moved to the neighborhood several years ago. All we'd grown back home in northern California were petunias and cucumbers. But on weekends, we'd driven out to the family farm and helped Grandpa pick ripe plump plums from the orchard or caught tadpoles in the irrigation ditch or fed the cows. Still, it was more novelty than work back then.

"Go to the meeting," my husband urged, "if only to meet some of our neighbors."

The meeting was held at the nearby elementary school. A woman handed out slips of paper.

"Give us your wish list," she said. "Tell us what you would like to grow in the garden."

Patience, peace, a better sense of community, I thought.

"Tomatoes, cucumbers, lettuce, basil, mint, snow peas, peppers, zucchini," I wrote.

Two years later I've come to know many of my fellow gardeners. We compare our work and trade seeds and secrets. We are young and old, Black and white, married and single. The neighborhood is no longer full of strangers.

Our little four-by-six plot has given me more than I could have ever guessed—a fresh harvest of tomatoes and lettuce and friendships, and the chance to grow.

REFLECTIONS

The Tomato Patch

FRAN YOUNGER

He will wipe away every tear from their eyes,
and death shall be no more, neither shall there be
mourning, nor crying, nor pain anymore,
for the former things have passed away.

REVELATION 21:4 (ESV)

No one knew Doris was dying; I certainly didn't. She wasn't outside in her garden as much as she usually was, didn't come along with me on hikes or picnics. Sometimes she made excuses, saying she was feeling tired or just getting over a cold. Maybe if I'd known that that was her last harvest, I would have canned all the tomatoes she gave me instead of dumping them out, over near the creek. But I was busy, they were overripe, and I needed to dig a new septic tank.

The backhoe came the same month Doris died. My heart wrenched each time its powerful teeth grasped one of the young trees and ripped it from the ground.

Lord, I prayed, *to lose my wooded view and my friend all at once is just too much.*

I tried to imagine what Doris would say—that the land would heal, that God would bring it back more glorious than it had been before.

"Just wait," I could almost hear her say.

But I was tired of waiting. I wanted Doris to be here with me, to tell me the names of the birds I saw out my window and the critters rushing through the brush. I wanted Doris to bring me the bounty from her garden. I wanted to go on walks with her down by the creek. I wanted her here to comfort me in my grief, impossible as that was.

Then one morning the following summer, I looked out my window and caught sight of a small red spot at the edge of the creek. I put on my boots and went down to investigate. Not until I came to the edge of the bank did I see it—a tangle of tomato vines spilling across the ground, right where I'd dumped those spoiled ones, the fruit of Doris's last crop. I could almost hear her saying in a near-whisper that even after a season of loss, God can heal—just as He makes dry land flourish again.

The glory of gardening: hands in the dirt, head in the sun, heart with nature. To nurture a garden is to feed not just the body, but the soul.

ALFRED AUSTIN

Weightier Matters

CYNTHIA RUCHTI

Woe to you, scribes and Pharisees, hypocrites! For you tithe mint and dill and cumin, and have neglected the weightier matters of the law: justice and mercy and faithfulness.

MATTHEW 23:23 (ESV)

My herb garden consists of a series of hanging baskets. I step onto my back deck to snip basil and thyme for the sauce simmering on the stove. Often, I pick rosemary for no other reason than the aroma it leaves on my hands. A few leaves of mint tossed into my giant water jug with fresh cucumbers and a squeeze of lime is more refreshing than anything the beverage aisle or soda machine can offer. I love my herbs.

And I know better than to plant mint in my raised beds or flat on the ground. Mint takes over. It grows—as they say—like a weed. It fares well in the hanging basket where I keep it contained.

I find it curious that the scribes and Pharisees—law keepers in Jesus's time who looked quizzically at Jesus and His spirit-of-the-law mentality—were faithful to give ten percent (or a tithe) of their mint and dill. Not exactly a sacrifice on their part. Mint no doubt grew like a weed in those days too.

They neglected what Jesus called "the weightier matters" of the law, however, which they claimed to follow with exacting diligence—justice and mercy and faithfulness. The Faithful One, Jesus, recognized unfaithfulness in their stinginess with the important things.

When I pass my basket of mint, I'm reminded of my responsibility to be generous with justice, mercy, and faithfulness.

I ask myself: *Am I giving abundantly of the things that matter?*

Lose yourself in generous service and every day can be a most unusual day, a triumphant day, an abundantly rewarding day!

WILLIAM ARTHUR WARD

Pruning Time

HEIDI GAUL

He cuts off every branch in me that bears no fruit, while every branch that does bear fruit he prunes so that it will be even more fruitful.

JOHN 15:2 (NIV)

Today I spent time outside pruning grapes, wisteria, and hydrangea—and remembering my parents. They were landscapers, and as they worked, I'd watch. The care and wisdom they displayed when tending plants fascinated me. *How could they know when and how much to trim off? Wouldn't it hurt the plant? Why were some bushes pruned so hard?*

I learned from them pruning techniques that seeped into my soul. Prune back to the joint to keep visual integrity. Cut on a slant to speed healing. Trim at the right time for that particular bush or vine so it doesn't go into shock and so it will blossom and bear fruit next season.

Years later, as an adult, I keep these tips tucked inside my mind like a treasure. When pruning my garden, I visualize my parents' hands guiding my own, and I feel their love.

Thanks to my mother and father, when Jesus disciplines me, I think about what He's doing. *Is He removing a hidden temptation, trimming me way back to the source? Is He freeing me from an unforgiven hurt, allowing me to heal and blossom again for Him? Have I reached a season where He wants me to address a tough issue I've long avoided?* All His pruning is necessary, even if it pains me at first.

I'm His blessed creation, one of His flowers. With His love, wisdom, and care, I can thrive and bloom to His glory.

REFLECTIONS

A Drop of Morning Dew

MELANIE BONNETTE SWANG

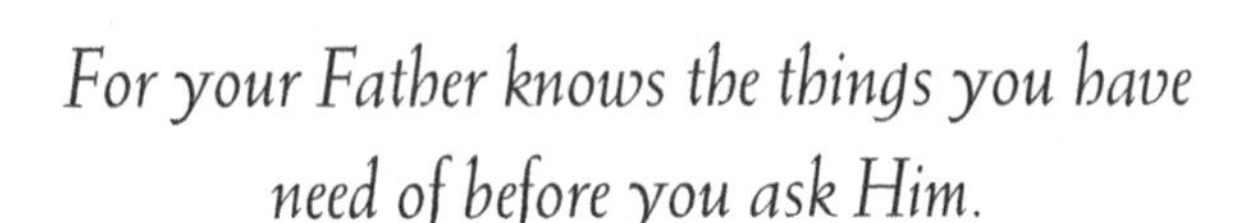

For your Father knows the things you have need of before you ask Him.

MATTHEW 6:8 (NKJV)

Early on a hot summer morning, I was on my hands and knees in the garden, pulling weeds. I stopped for a moment to wipe my brow. I'd hoped that if I started early enough that day I'd escape some of the heat and humidity. But even at this hour, I was sweltering.

Sure wish I'd remembered to grab my bandanna! It is a special one designed to cool its wearer. Simply insert a couple of ice cubes into a compartment sewn inside, tie it around your neck, and voilà!—the ice melts and drips down your back.

I should go inside and get it, I thought. But then I looked down at my clothes; they were covered in dirt. *Maybe not.*

I got up and walked over to the tall, dense patch of ginger growing alongside the house. I plopped down in the shade and immediately felt a trickle of cool water run down my back. Startled, I turned quickly and laughed out loud. I'd sat in just the right spot, disturbing a ginger leaf still cradling its morning dew.

That moment of refreshment reminded me of how much God lovingly cares for me, no matter where I am.

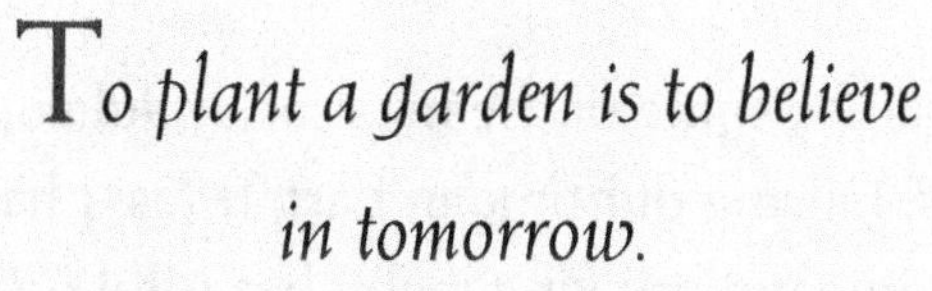

To plant a garden is to believe in tomorrow.

AUDREY HEPBURN

Wayward Vines

CATHY BRYANT

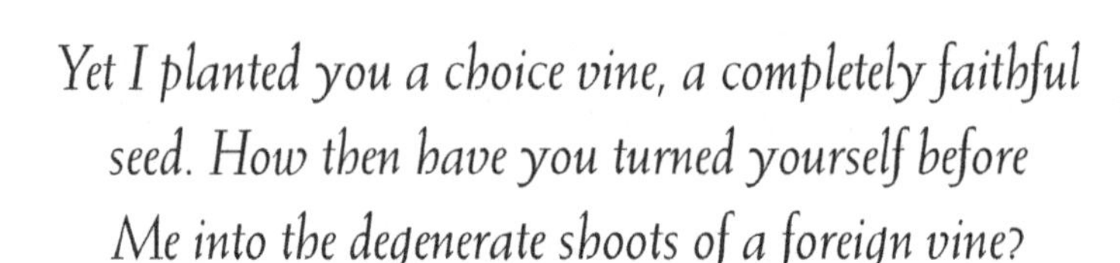

Yet I planted you a choice vine, a completely faithful seed. How then have you turned yourself before Me into the degenerate shoots of a foreign vine?

JEREMIAH 2:21 (NASB1995)

Vines can be some of the most beautiful and productive plants. During our time in East Texas, I had the privilege of seeing and growing many beautiful ones. Among them were wisteria, honeysuckle, morning glories, climbing roses, and—to my own detriment—trumpet vine.

I distinctly remember a phone conversation with my mom soon after I planted that vine and mentioned it in the course of our conversation.

"You'll never get rid of it," she said.

She was right.

The trumpet vine grows wherever it pleases. There's no training it. To make matters even worse, it sends out shoots underground, quickly taking over a much bigger area than the gardener ever intended.

Many times in the Bible, God refers to people as His vineyard. When we stay connected to Him, we can produce much for Him and His kingdom. Unfortunately, vines also can—and often do—shoot off in their own direction, unruly and wandering.

For His part, God brings wayward vines back under His control and care. But if we persist in going our own way, He just might allow it like He did with the nation of Israel. Though they were His chosen people, He allowed them to be taken into captivity because of their waywardness.

When I sense myself growing away from Him—when I get disconnected from the Vine—I do all I can to submit my life to His tending. It is truly the only way to a blessed and productive life.

Lord Jesus, thank You for being the Vine. Only through You can I find nourishment, sustenance, and productivity. God, thank You for being the Gardener of my soul, who tends me in ways I won't be able to fully comprehend this side of heaven. In the name of Jesus, I pray. Amen.

The earth laughs in flowers.

RALPH WALDO EMERSON

God's Tender Love

MARION BOND WEST

As the deer longs for streams of water,
so I long for you, O God.

PSALM 42:1 (NLT)

A trip to the gym had left me depleted. Everyone looked younger than me—and more athletic. I felt out of place, spent. Picturing my return home, I dreaded trudging in the front door, dropping into a chair, my soul and body so weary.

What was even worse was that God seemed so far away.

The sun was Georgia hot, even at eleven in the morning, as I exited the building. Discouragement tagged along with me.

A woman passed me, walking briskly to the parking area. When she stopped several feet in front of me and took out a bottle of water, I slowed down and pretended to rummage through my gym bag. After removing the cap to her water bottle, she leaned way over and singled out one red zinnia in the garden that grew beside the iron fence. Carefully, even lovingly, she gave that flower a drink.

As I watched her, an amazing thing happened. It felt as though someone had poured joy directly into my soul, just as deliberately and carefully as she had poured water on that bloom, that one flower in all the hundreds.

After the woman straightened up and walked to her car, I lingered by the red zinnia. Somehow, I felt refreshed, as though God had reached down to earth and touched me.

"I see you, Marion," He seemed to say. "I love you."

Father, I silently prayed, *You find such tender ways to show Yourself to me when I need You most. Thank You!*

REFLECTIONS

Walking in the Garden

CANDEE FICK

And they heard the sound of the LORD God walking in the garden in the cool of the day, and the man and his wife hid themselves from the presence of the LORD God among the trees of the garden.

GENESIS 3:8 (ESV)

For the past five summers, our family has spent a week in Branson, Missouri. In addition to boating on and swimming in Table Rock Lake, we get passes to Silver Dollar City, an amusement park. Lining the edges of pathways wrapped in and around the rides, shows, and shops are a lush variety of plants. I know that the higher humidity and lower altitude play a big role in producing such bounty, but that doesn't stop me from pausing to admire the colorful foliage and flowers surrounded by tall shade trees.

These garden patches remind me of a time during my college days in Tulsa, Oklahoma. Just months before graduation, I discovered a garden-like park hidden away in a neighborhood near where I was student-teaching. Paths wound between bushes and flowerbeds all in bloom. Overhead, trees bore new leaves, and birds filled the air with singing as sweet as the aroma of the blossoms.

The garden beckoned and I longed to spend hours meandering to explore every corner. If only there had been a special someone to walk with hand-in-hand, sharing our dreams and whispering the secrets of our hearts. Simply walking and talking in the garden in the cool of the day.

Yet, there *was* someone with me. And there still is. God has been with me all along.

God longs to spend time with us. He wants to walk around with us every day. Just like back in the Garden of Eden, He comes "walking in the garden in the cool in the day" (Genesis 3:8, ESV). It's up to us whether we will come out of hiding and keep in step with Him.

A family vacation at a crowded amusement park reminded me of how much I long to spend time walking in the garden with God. I wonder which path we'll take and what we'll talk about today.

REFLECTIONS

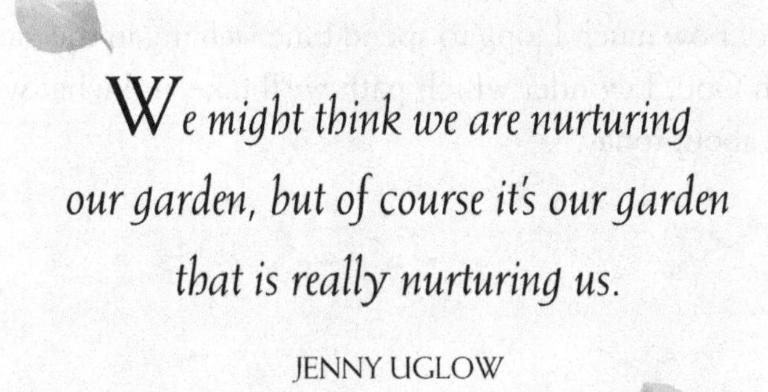

We might think we are nurturing our garden, but of course it's our garden that is really nurturing us.

JENNY UGLOW

Miracle Flower

MARY LOU CARNEY

I am the L*ORD, the God of all mankind. Is anything too hard for me?*

JEREMIAH 32:27 (NIV)

In March, sixteen years ago, my mother died. I was devastated, numb. My friend Aline sent me a lovely pink hydrangea, top-heavy in its small clay pot, and I vowed to keep this plant alive. For weeks it bloomed on my desk before the ground was warm enough for outdoor planting.

Slowly, flowers began to appear: the first year, only one; the next year, two. Some years I'm blessed with more blossoms than I can count; other times the blooms are sparse.

Recently, I mentioned to a gardener friend how special this plant is to me. He looked at me as if I were crazy.

"That thing should never have survived even one winter! It's a hothouse florist's plant. It was never meant to face up to this frigid Midwest weather!"

Today I walked outside, noting the approaching end of summer. I caught a glimpse of my hydrangea bush. The pink blossoms had faded to a mottled mauvy green, but they were still lovely. I picked a handful and brought them inside. They will dry quite well and last through the snowy months, a lovely reminder of Mother—and miracles.

Shelter

KEN SAMPSON

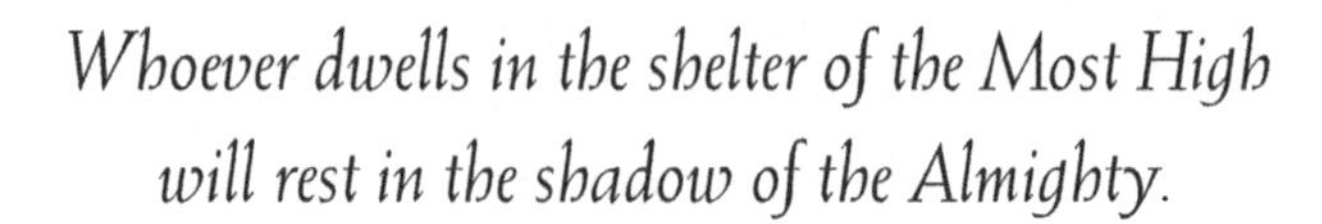

Whoever dwells in the shelter of the Most High will rest in the shadow of the Almighty.

PSALM 91:1 (NIV)

On a recent midsummer day, I pulled the garden hose to the corner of our home to water a basket of hanging red geraniums. A startled commotion interrupted my morning chore when a white speckled fawn bolted from under a nearby wild raspberry bush and dashed across the lawn. The sound of scampering hoofs indicated I'd disturbed the shelter of this baby deer.

Bending over to look under the raspberry branches, I saw what looked to be a well-protected fort. A right-angle concrete foundation and porch enclosure formed the backdrop. Offshoots of the prickly bush provided camouflage cover. It was an expert hideaway.

I, too, have an expert hideaway: God, who offers me His protection.

Whatever the ups and downs of the day, I remain confident and secure. A safe retreat in God's reliable hands shelters me come what may. As I believe this comforting verse, and take refuge in Him, I go forward in peace.

"TO A FRIEND WHO SENT ME SOME ROSES"

BY JOHN KEATS

As late I rambled in the happy fields,
What time the sky-lark shakes the tremulous dew
From his lush clover covert;—when anew
Adventurous knights take up their dinted shields:
I saw the sweetest flower wild nature yields,
A fresh-blown musk-rose; 'twas the first that threw
Its sweets upon the summer: graceful it grew
As is the wand that queen Titania wields.
And, as I feasted on its fragrancy,
I thought the garden-rose it far excell'd:
But when, O Wells! thy roses came to me
My sense with their deliciousness was spell'd:
Soft voices had they, that with tender plea
Whisper'd of peace, and truth,
and friendliness unquell'd.

My Rooftop Garden

MARGARET SANGSTER

The eyes of your understanding being enlightened; that you may know what is the hope of His calling, what are the riches of the glory of His inheritance in the saints.

EPHESIANS 1:18 (NKJV)

My first garden grew on the terrace of a rooftop apartment, twenty-two stories above a busy city avenue. Instead of springing from the warm brown earth, it rose from wooden boxes filled with soil by the neighborhood florist. This first garden brought me comfort and peace and, eventually, a glimpse of glory.

It came to me when I was resentful and hurt after the death of my husband—a young and talented artist. I took up gardening because it was something I had never done before, and it carried no ache of a shared memory. I also hoped that the labor of gardening, even on a small scale, would make me tired enough to sleep at night.

Automatically, I dug holes in the dirt and poked seeds in them. While I dug and planted, I was tempted to forget the whole thing, and yet, because I had always tried to finish the projects I started, I plodded on.

But it wasn't until my garden showed life that I became aware of the effort it was making to give me pleasure.

When I saw tender shoots rising through the ground—when my garden was slightly over a month old—I laughed aloud. The green shoots, feeling their way blindly out of the ground, were like baby kittens whose eyes hadn't opened. They made me feel stronger, lighter. Almost immediately I felt the tears standing in my eyes. Healing tears.

The seeds I'd planted were responding to my summons, and there was something in their response that awakened a protective instinct in me.

After a hard rain, my attention was drawn to the shoots that earlier had seemed so slender and fragile. Although the rain beat them close to earth, it didn't break them. They bent, but they did not break. Instinctively I knew that when another day dawned and another sun shone, they would be able to lift their faces to the sky.

It would be the first of many lessons my garden taught me, and maybe the most important: Adversity might bend the spirit, but the spirit need not break.

The Benefits of Pruning

CATHY BRYANT

The steadfast of mind You will keep in perfect peace,
Because he trusts in You. Trust in the LORD forever,
For in GOD the LORD, we have *an everlasting Rock.*

ISAIAH 26:3–4 (NASB)

Pruning is a necessary part of gardening. Any seasoned gardener can tell you about the benefits of cutting back plants—and about the consequences of not doing so.

On tomatoes, pinching off suckers (growth in between two sturdy branches) can result in a stronger plant and bigger fruit. Deadheading flowers can ensure a longer-blooming plant. Removing the seed heads on vegetables will allow the current fruit to grow larger. Pruning back a fruit tree not only makes the shape of the tree more attractive but also results in larger fruit.

When the Lord does careful pruning in my life, I don't always welcome it. I naturally balk at any kind of cutting away from my life because I don't like to think that I need any improvement or growth. I don't like to experience suffering, even if I know or can at least trust that it's beneficial in the long-term.

But just as plants need pruning, so do I. I need to remember that it is much better to experience a season of pruning to mature me and make me more fruitful than it is to be severed from the vine or to wither and die.

God prunes us all to make us more fruitful. When we accept His pruning with great joy, knowing that each thing He cuts away is nonessential, He makes us more like Christ—and more fruitful for the Kingdom.

Father God, thank You for the hard work of Your pruning in my life. I confess I don't necessarily like the process. But I can't argue with the results! Teach me to welcome Your pruning. Amen.

~ Deadhead Your Days ~

Deadheading is the horticultural practice of removing dead or shriveled flowers from plants. It's a form of pruning and makes the plant healthier and more beautiful.

What parts of your life might be like dead or faded blooms? How could pruning certain habits, relationships, or unhealthy thoughts out of your heart and mind allow you to grow stronger? Ask God for wisdom as you consider discarding unhelpful parts of your life and look with hope on the new growth that will come.

Weeding Your Life

CANDEE FICK

Search me, God, and know my heart; test me and know my anxious thoughts. See if there is any offensive way in me, and lead me in the way everlasting.

PSALM 139:23–24 (NIV)

With rich, nutritious soil and enough water and sunshine, what do you think grows in my garden? Very hardy weeds, that's what!

Although my youngest son loves to pick pretty yellow dandelion flowers, I'm destined to crawl around on my hands and knees, trying to get to the roots to make sure they never show their mocking faces in my garden or yard again. Whether I use a hoe or a hand spade, I am on a mission to get rid of the weeds before they take over. Week after week, I wage war.

I can't help wondering as I weed my garden: *What are the weeds in my spiritual life? Are there activities that distract me, competing for my time and energy and space when I could be doing more for the Lord? Emotions that wrap me up in a tangle of bitterness and resentment? Materialistic or envious attitudes that crop up?*

I want to be honest. I don't think I'm always as diligent in weeding out my life as I am about keeping my garden free from weeds. I need to keep at it, digging deep to expose the roots. When I relax and fail to keep vigilant, they creep back in. And so I pray:

Dear God, You know my heart. I ask that You keep showing me what I need to weed out of my life so I can better love and serve You. Amen.

A man's mind may be likened to a garden, which may be intelligently cultivated or allowed to run wild; but whether cultivated or neglected, it must, and will, bring forth. If no useful seeds are put into it, then an abundance of useless weed-seeds will fall therein, and will continue to produce their kind. Just as a gardener cultivates his plot . . . so a man may tend the garden of his mind, weeding out all the wrong, useless, and impure thoughts . . . [A] man sooner or later discovers that he is the master-gardener of his soul, the director of his life.

JAMES ALLEN, "EFFECT OF THOUGHT ON CIRCUMSTANCES,"
FROM *AS A MAN THINKETH*, 1908

Overflowing Goodness

SUSANNA FOTH AUGHTMON

Jesus answered, "Everyone who drinks this water will be thirsty again, but whoever drinks the water I give them will never thirst. Indeed, the water I give them will become in them a spring of water welling up to eternal life."

JOHN 4:13–14 (NIV)

I live in California, and every decade or so we experience drought. The rain stops. The hills turn brown. Summer brush fires break out. And cities clamp down on water usage. Residents are asked to let their front lawns suffer to save water. Instead of having lush green patches of grass lining the streets, everyone starts cultivating rock gardens and succulents to keep their properties looking well-tended.

Water is precious. Water is life. And Jesus is the Living Water. We need a constant flow of His love and grace to nurture growth. We need His refreshing truth and life-altering forgiveness. The overflow of His goodness lets us flourish in every way.

There have been long seasons in my life when my faith has felt dry and dusty. Hope has hardened into doubt. Grief, financial difficulties, and the general stresses of life have drained me of His presence. I have felt like my spirit is one of those parched patches of California earth.

But Jesus never looks at my hard heart and says, "Oh man, she will never grow again." He never says, "I'm done with her. She has failed Me one too many times."

Instead, He says, "I am right here. Come find Me and never thirst again."

Jesus is all about life, restoration, and new growth. Dry seasons are a part of this life. But He is always waiting to fill me up with His refreshing presence.

When you do things from your soul, you feel a river moving in you, a joy.

RUMI

Tending My Faith

JEFF CHU

For we live by faith, not by sight.

2 CORINTHIANS 5:7 (NIV)

I've noticed something about my generation, especially those of us who grew up in the suburbs: We want to grow things. Sometimes we'll sit in our yardless New York City apartments and dream about being farmers, raising chickens or cultivating herbs.

I have a little house in the country where, every month or so, I can escape from the city for a few days, buy a couple of bags of potting soil, and get closer to realizing that fantasy. There's a garden patch out back where a random selection of plants—raspberries, a little rhubarb, some chives—were planted years ago. Last spring, I was up at the house for a week and decided to experiment with a few more things. I added some thyme, some rosemary and cucumber, peppers, and chard.

Well, I'm no gentleman farmer. Those of you who are more familiar with growing things may laugh, but on a subsequent visit, I learned that my little plants were still mostly, well, little. The thyme and rosemary turned out to be hardy, but the cucumbers were small and malformed; the pepper plants had become breakfast, lunch, and dinner for bugs; and I had enough chard to make the garnish for one plate. Even the raspberries were only producing tiny amounts of fruit.

I realized that my plants needed regular tending—and occasionally special care. That little epiphany led to another realization: My garden patch is rather like my spiritual life. I get complacent, busy, lazy. I'm lax about prayer. I'm inconsistent about reading my Bible.

And then I wonder why I feel far away from God.

It's been a hectic time at work and in the city, so I'm heading back to my country place soon. During my few days there, I've resolved that I'll prune those raspberry plants and spend some time tending to my faith, giving it some of the attention it needs to get back to good growth.

Only You, Lord, can grow my faith—and my garden.

REFLECTIONS

The Promise of Protection

CANDEE FICK

And the peace of God, which transcends all understanding, will guard your hearts and your minds in Christ Jesus.

PHILIPPIANS 4:7 (NIV)

Have you ever read the book *Peter Rabbit* by Beatrix Potter? That mischievous bunny just can't resist the lure of Mr. McGregor's garden and his lettuces, carrots, beans, and radishes. It's a feast worth crawling under a gate for—even though he gets chased around by an angry gardener with a rake for doing so.

Part of gardening involves putting up some type of barrier to protect the plants from outside invaders. These range from children's and dogs' trampling feet to munching deer to pecking birds and chewing insects. Wise gardeners put up fences and cover fruit trees with nets. They may choose to thwart the bad bugs with insecticides, friendly bugs, or by other means.

It makes me wonder: *How do I guard my heart against spiritual invaders of worry and fear? Do I let the insects of doubt eat away at my faith? How do I build a wall of truth? Cover myself with hope? Grow patience and gentleness and joy?*

One of my favorite passages in the Bible is Philippians 4:7. We're told not to be anxious about anything and are assured that God's peace will guard our hearts.

Do you see that promise, that powerful word? *Guard*. God's peace guards us as though we're in a fortress, surrounded by a moat, hidden away. He protects us so that, like a well-tended garden, we can bloom and bear fruit.

Everything that slows us down and forces patience, everything that sets us back into the slow circles of nature, is a help. Gardening is an instrument of grace.

MAY SARTON

Abuela's Garden

CARMEN ESCAMILLA

Hear me, O Lord, for Your lovingkindness is *good; turn to me according to the multitude of Your tender mercies.*

PSALM 69:16 (NKJV)

Maybe gardening wasn't the best plan for the day after all. The sun was broiling hot.

"Let's go to the movies," my son, Juan, said. "Where it's air-conditioned."

My daughter, Monica, held up her doll. "It's too hot for us too!"

I wasn't any more enthusiastic than they were about tending my mother's garden. *What was I thinking even suggesting it?* We'd been living with Mom since my divorce. My garden, that home, that life—all of it was gone now.

"Maybe we should go to the movies," I said. "We can help Abuela with her garden next season."

Before the children had a chance to reply, Mom came out the back door with a tray of lemonade and cookies.

"Look what I have for my three farmers!" she said.

She handed me a napkin. *"Dios es bueno,"* she said, as she so often did. "God is good."

Mom was always saying that, especially in my despair. It had been weeks since we moved in, and I wasn't doing any better. Sadness and guilt overwhelmed me. I stared at the shriveled carrot seeds in my hand.

"Let's get started," said Mom.

I grabbed a hoe and chopped at the ground. "Lord, till my own heart, and remove the hard places within it," I whispered.

Monica practiced counting out the right number of seeds. Juan made sure each row was labeled. Monica started singing a song she'd learned at school. Soon all of us were singing along as we worked.

When we finished, I breathed in the smell of fresh, wet earth. It's done, I thought. A new life for the garden and a new life for us. It was my first fleeting moment of hope in a long, long time.

In the fall, we had a harvest beyond what I could have hoped. Pumpkins, carrots, zucchini. Carrying in an armload of pumpkins one day, Mom smiled at me and said, *"Dios es bueno."*

I nodded and agreed. "Yes," I said. "God *is* good."

The Moonflower

SHARI SMYTH

He will wipe every tear from their eyes. There will be no more death or mourning or crying or pain, for the old order of things has passed away.

REVELATION 21:4 (NIV)

One summer Sunday morning after the early service, I was in the side garden of our church pulling up a few weeds when I noticed a woman of about fifty who was new to our congregation. She was studying a plate-sized, cloud-white bloom on a sturdy vine.

"What is the name of this flower?" she asked with an urgency that drew me to her side.

"It's a moonflower," I said. "It only blooms once and always at night. It has the most wonderful fragrance," I added, bending down to breathe in its perfume.

"Oh," she said, "Moonflower! That's it! All these years I'd forgotten. But just now this wonderful memory's come back. I was about three when my mother planted one of these. She waited and waited for it to bloom. Every night she'd go out and check and come inside disappointed. Then one night she rushed into the house all excited, pulled Dad and me out to the garden, and pointed to this exquisite white flower standing out against the darkness.

I can still see Mom's face that night and hear her saying over and over, 'It was worth the wait.'"

The woman touched the flower.

"Isn't it amazing how a memory can bring someone back?"

She left with a spring in her step. I went back to my weeding, pondering this gift from a fragile moonflower on its way to dust.

Thank You, Father, for sudden blooms of memory that, while they cannot last, refresh me on my journey toward my everlasting home. Amen.

Summertime is always the best of what might be.

CHARLES BOWDEN

A Reminder

BILL GIOVANNETTI

The grass withers, the flower fades, but the word of our God stands forever.

ISAIAH 40:8 (NKJV)

I looked over our landscaped gardens with both sadness and pride. Pride, because they were beautiful; sadness, because I knew that something had to die.

Every plant had been selected by my wife and me. Every shrub, every tree, every flower had been placed strategically. Each one told the story of design and labor. In our rocky soil, these extensive plantings required a rented jackhammer to dig a hole big enough for each root ball. It was backbreaking work, but it was worth it. After years of sweat equity, our planting areas looked absolutely beautiful.

In our first year in northern California, it rained every day for a month in the winter, and then we experienced a hot, dry summer. The pattern continued, and this made for verdant landscaping.

But now we had to decide which plants would need to die. We were facing a major drought; we actually were several years into it, with no end in sight. Water restrictions required us to turn off the irrigation, to rethink our landscape, and to say goodbye to that hard-won beauty.

As I walked through our yard for early morning devotions, I heard God whisper to me. He reminded me that all things on earth will pass away, that I'm a pilgrim here. This brief sojourn will give way to heavenly glory, where the rivers of God never run dry, where His beauty lasts forever.

Father of Mercies, teach me to hold all earthly things lightly and to fix my mind on a realm where Your grace will never fade. Amen.

~ See Your Connectedness ~

A garden does more than add beauty. All plants—even little shrubs or the humblest potted herbs—take in and trap greenhouse gases that can cause global warming. They then release clean, fresh air into the atmosphere.

In what ways might *your* presence in your home, neighborhood, or community be like a healthy plant, helping to clear the air for other people and living things? Even in small ways, you, too, are making the world a healthier place.

Weeds of Worry

KERI WYATT KENT

For the Spirit God gave us does not make us timid, but gives us power, love and self-discipline.

2 TIMOTHY 1:7 (NIV)

I love to garden, but weeding? Not so much. However, weeding is an essential part of gardening. Weeds grow right next to my tomatoes and flowers, and if left alone, will eventually cause destruction. Unchecked, they'll keep a garden from being fruitful.

Jesus said that the seeds of truth He plants in our hearts get crowded out by worries, as well as by our desire for wealth or status. I can honestly say I don't wish I were rich, but I wish we had a little more. Not a lot, just a bit more. When things are tight, I worry about our financial security. *How will we manage to pay for college? Will my husband find a new job?* These worries are weeds that strangle out joy.

I should also admit that, in a random hour of almost any day, I probably have a dozen other worries flit through my brain. I don't consciously *decide* to worry; in fact, I try not to. But still, the cares of this life march right on through.

Jesus is the only one who can give me the fruitful life I long for. I can get it by opening my life to Him, letting Him pull the weeds of worry and covetousness while cultivating contentment and trust in me.

"LIVE THY LIFE"

BY FLORENCE EARLE COATES

Live thy life gallantly and undismayed:
Whatever harms may hide within the shade,
Be thou of fear, my spirit! more afraid.

In earthly pathways evil springeth rife;
But dread not thou, too much, or pain or strife
That plunge thee to the greater depths of life!

What though the storm-cloud holds the bolt that sears?
The eagle of the crag, that nothing fears,
Still, still is young after a hundred years!

Paying It Forward

MELODY BONNETTE SWANG

Every good gift and every perfect gift is from above, coming down from the Father of lights, with whom there is no variation or shadow due to change."

JAMES 1:17 (ESV)

Recently, a neighbor and I got together at my house for iced tea. She said she wanted advice about which flowers to plant in her garden. Glasses of tea in hand, we strolled through my yard.

"These pink knockout roses and azaleas grow well," I said. "And planting annuals, like dianthus and impatiens, will keep your yard full of color."

We then went around back where I had planted a combination of purple agapanthus and bright yellow lantana. She pointed to a spot in the corner where four-foot-high green stalks were planted. They were bare, except for a few small leaves.

"What happened there?" she asked.

"Oh, that's milkweed," I replied.

She went closer.

"Oh no," she exclaimed, "caterpillars are eating it!"

"I know," I said, laughing.

"Don't you mind?" she asked.

"No," I said. "They're monarch caterpillars. Every year, butterflies lay their eggs on the milkweed, and then caterpillars hatch. They'll cocoon and eventually emerge as beautiful butterflies."

"But they've eaten all the flowers!" she said.

"That's okay," I replied. "The way I see it, every flower in my garden is a gift from God, and helping to sustain monarch butterflies is a simple way to pay His gift forward."

As we walked back to the house for more tea, I said a silent word of thanks to God for His many gifts.

Never be afraid to trust an unknown future to a known God.

CORRIE TEN BOOM

A Trip to the Farmers' Market

JEANETTE LEVELLIE

Those who sow with tears will reap with songs of joy.

PSALM 126:5 (NIV)

When health issues forced me to give up working in my beloved vegetable garden, I mourned. I loved pulling funny-shaped carrots from the soil. I loved the smell of tomato plants on my hands. I loved kneeling in the warm earth as I weeded, butterflies dancing around my face.

But when back pain and the cost of chiropractic visits increased; I knew it was time to retire as a gardener. It was a grim reality, but I had to face it.

This summer, I traded my vegetable seed packets and wheelbarrow for potted flowers and tomato plants. Although I was excited to watch these grow and bloom, I still missed my vegetable plot and working in the dirt to grow my own produce.

Then I remembered the weekly farmers' market on our town square. Family farms and individual gardeners, artists, and others sell produce and crafts from card tables and the beds of pickup trucks. Not only do we get to purchase local, fresh vegetables and fruit every Saturday, but we also have the treat of making new friends and chatting with people we have known for years.

I no longer grow the vegetables I use in my salads and stews. That is a joy I must savor only in my memory, and I hope to do again in heaven. Still, Jesus compensated for my loss by giving me a new form of joy, gathering with neighbors and other members of my community in the town square.

When we experience loss, we may be tempted to think we'll never find another person, hobby, church, or job to take the former one's place. It's true, we won't. But if we open our hearts to the new beginnings Jesus provides; He will enrich us with experiences that delight and surprise us.

He is the Master Gardener, willing to share His bounty with all.

REFLECTIONS

Time for Thinning

CANDEE FICK

"Everything is permissible," but not everything is beneficial. "Everything is permissible," but not everything builds up.

1 CORINTHIANS 10:23 (CSB)

The hardest gardening task for me is thinning. If you're not familiar with the term, "thinning" means that when gardeners grow vegetables from seed, they pull or cut the extra and weakest seedlings until they have the right number of plants at the correct spacing.

Even though I know I need to do this, I detest thinning. I hate pulling up perfectly good carrots or cucumber plants or pinching blossoms off pumpkin and watermelon vines. It feels wrong; it's not like they're weeds!

If I leave too many plants in a small area, though, none of them will grow to their full potential. They'll compete for nutrients and space. And a single vine can't put energy into a dozen melons. By thinning, I allow my garden to maximize its resources for the greatest yield.

I face the same problem in my own life. While I can set up protective barriers and yank up weeds, I have a difficult time saying "No" to good activities. There's nothing wrong with singing in the choir, leading a Bible study, working a part-time job, driving my kids to various activities, scrapbooking, exercising, or doing yard work. Nothing wrong, that is, unless I'm stretched so thin that I have to short-change one area to juggle the next. If you're like me, it's often sleep that I skimp on when I'm doing too much. And getting too little sleep is never a good idea.

When I'm exhausted and overwhelmed, I realize that it's time to do a little thinning. Even the "good" must make way for the "best" in my life. I pray for wisdom as I reevaluate the tasks in different seasons of life and decide which "plants" need to be pulled. I thin out my schedule for a bit, during the summer—choir, for example—when garden and yard work require a lot of time and attention. And I grow healthier in my faith for it.

God, help me to remember to leave room around the margins and to keep my schedule thinned out so that I have time to spend with You. Amen.

Mom's Clippers

SUSANNA FOTH AUGHTMON

Trust in the Lord with all your heart and lean not on your own understanding; in all your ways submit to him, and he will make your paths straight.

PROVERBS 3:5–6 (NIV)

My mom is a gardener to her very core. I joke that if you cut her, she will bleed green! Whenever she comes to visit, I ask for her help in my garden, and she is always willing.

We come back from the nursery, laden with annuals, perennials, and a variety of fertilizers. Before we start to plant or prep the soil, she takes time to deadhead the rosebush that she planted near our shed four years ago. She is ruthless with those clippers. There is not a wilting bloom left on it when she is done.

She tells me, "If you keep pruning your roses throughout the summer, they will keep coming back."

She's right. It seems when those dead blooms are still on the bush, they still suck the life out of the plant. Once the dead flowers are gone, the rosebush can put all of its energy into forcing new luscious blooms open to soak up the sun. Each year the old-fashioned blooms are larger and more fragrant than the ones the year before. Pruning yields glorious blooms.

Somehow I am the one being pruned, by God. And I don't enjoy it. I would rather ignore all the dead places in my life because pruning is painful. What I never seem to remember is that they are sucking the life right out of me. When I keep those rotting areas festering in my life, I am less fruitful. My life's growth is stunted unless I allow the Gardener to do His holy work in me.

Jesus would have me living my life to the full, getting all I need from the Vine, growing, changing, and become more like Him daily.

When I watch my mom and her shears, I'm reminded again of my loving Gardener who prunes me for my own good.

REFLECTIONS

Hibiscus Seeds

MIKE FREZON

Consider how the wild flowers grow. They do not labor or spin. Yet I tell you, not even Solomon in all his splendor was dressed like one of these.

LUKE 12:27 (NIV)

After I retired, I decided to attend to a task I'd been avoiding: cleaning out our hundred-year-old garage. The day I began that chore, I pushed at the garage's wooden doors, but they were as stubbornly stuck as I felt in this new stage of my life.

Inside, I picked my way past coolers, snow shovels, and folded tarps. Here I was, puttering, of all things. I raised my eyes to the rafters, where cobwebs hung like hazy film. *God, is this what it's come to? Do You still have a use for me?*

At one point, I was clearing off a shelf when my hand hit something hard. I pulled out a grungy, round metal tin. I wondered, *Could this old tin hold a hidden fortune?*

Little by little, I loosened the cover until it popped off and clanked to the ground. Inside were several yellowed envelopes. I opened one, and my heart sank.

Peg, my wife, poked her head inside the garage door. "What's that?"

"Seeds," I said. Nothing but seeds. We then found a letter dated May 13, 1940, addressed to the original owner of our house.

"I am sending you the seeds of the hibiscus you admired when you stopped at our tourist home last year," Peg read. "Plant when the ground becomes warm, and do not be alarmed if they do not come up for several weeks—they are slow to germinate."

"Huh," I said. "Eighty years old. I wonder if they'll still grow." I grabbed a garden tray, shook the seeds out of the envelope, pushed them into the soil, and set the tray in the sun.

Six weeks later, I happened to notice the tray. There in the damp soil, a sprig of green had emerged. *Was it grass? A weed? Or could it be . . . ?*

I found myself checking first thing every morning until one day I saw leaves that looked just like the illustration of a hibiscus plant I'd found online.

It was then I realized that just like the little hibiscus, with God's help, I would keep growing and bloom again too.

A Summer Storm

TIFFANY DUFFER-DUNAWAY

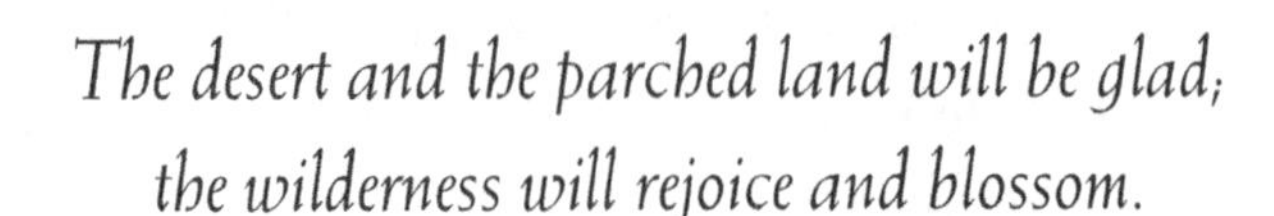

The desert and the parched land will be glad;
the wilderness will rejoice and blossom.

ISAIAH 35:1 (NIV)

I drove home, navigating fallen branches. A violent summer storm had hit just before I'd left work—thunder, lightning, rain, and terrible winds. Debris was strewn everywhere. It wasn't so much our house that concerned me, but our garden. I worried about the low-hanging branch of an old oak tree over our flower bed.

Just the day before, my husband, David, and I had been sitting outside, enjoying the cool evening air, when he pointed up at the bough.

"If that falls," he said, "it could crush everything."

That garden meant the world to me. As a girl, I'd always thought having a flower bed in front made a home look happy.

Life had thrown us more than a few curveballs. David had Type 1 diabetes, but he'd managed the symptoms well enough through diet, insulin, and monitoring his blood-sugar levels. Then one day, I had to rush him to the hospital after he fell into a diabetic coma. He was quickly airlifted to another facility for proper treatment. Doctors there warned that he might wake up with brain damage—if he woke up at all. A week later, David walked out of that hospital.

Although David didn't have quite the energy he once had, he still had the green thumb he'd inherited from his grandfathers. Pacing himself, David dug, planted, watered, and pruned. Then came that summer storm, as violent as any I've seen.

As I pulled into the driveway, I could see that the bough had crashed right on top of the flower bed, just as David had warned.

I took a deep breath and got out of the car to inspect the damage. I peered between the oak leaves. The marigolds smiled back at me, the daylilies hadn't even been nicked, the hostas held their heads high, the petunias weren't crushed.

Somehow the branch had fallen in such a way that it created a *bridge* over the flower bed—protecting, not destroying, it. I walked around in amazement. Not a flower had been injured; not a petal was damaged.

"God, You are so good," I whispered. "Thank You for Your protection too."

My Bumper Crop

LINDA WELLS

Ask and it will be given to you; seek and you will find; knock and the door will be opened to you.

MATTHEW 7:7 (NIV)

Last summer, my garden provided more vegetables than my family could eat.

"Wayne, would you take these to your youth group tonight?" I asked my son.

"Aw, Mom!" he said, with a grimace. Making an entrance with a basket of tomatoes, peppers, and squash wouldn't look too cool, I guess.

Still, I couldn't bear the thought of them going to waste. I had class later. Maybe someone there would want them.

Class ended and the teacher asked if anyone had any questions. I raised my hand.

"This isn't about homework," I said, "but would anyone like some veggies?"

I had no takers. I was gathering my books to leave when a classmate stopped me.

"I would like the produce," she said quietly. "I ran out of grocery money, and I prayed for fresh produce."

My garden helped to answer someone's prayer. Now *that* was pretty cool.

"PRAYER"

BY GEORGE MACDONALD

We doubt the word that tells us: Ask,
And ye shall have your prayer;
We turn our thoughts as to a task,
With will constrained and rare.

And yet we have; these scanty prayers
Yield gold without alloy:
O God, but he that trusts and dares
Must have a boundless joy!

Weeding with My Father

ERIN MACPHERSON

Each of you should use whatever gift you have received to serve others, as faithful stewards of God's grace in its various forms.

1 PETER 4:10 (NIV)

Pulling weeds is my Dad's love language. Suffice it to say, it's not mine—especially in Texas, where stalks grow six feet tall and bugs swarm every leaf as I struggle to yank out the roots from the unforgiving clay. It's a chore I do only when absolutely necessary, which wasn't today.

I was taking a much-needed break while my mom graciously watched the kids. So, I sat on her front porch, sipping a tall glass of iced tea, and took a deep breath of the spring air, ripe with the smell of the just-blossomed china-berry trees. As my eyes scanned the bright coral trumpet vines that lined my parents' garden fence, I caught a glimpse of my father, crouched in his rose garden, painstakingly pulling the tangled vines that threatened his precious plants.

My breath caught in my throat, as memories washed over me.

This was the man who had so indulgently attended every one of my track meets when I was in high school, sprinting across the field so he could cheer me on at both ends of the track. This was the man who paced the hospital waiting room as each of my children was born, eager to meet yet another sprout on his growing family tree. This was the man who hoists my kids up onto his shoulders and lets them look out from the vantage point of a giant. This man gave me life and so much more.

I stood up and grabbed some gloves.

"Hey, Dad, may I help you?" I called.

He flashed a big toothy smile.

"Of course!" he replied. "This one here needs two pairs of hands to pull it out."

All throughout my life, my dad has shown me how my Heavenly Father loves us—selflessly, fully, and mercifully. I was so grateful to be able to do something small for him in return.

REFLECTIONS

The Problem with Neglect

CANDEE FICK

Still others are like the seeds sown among the thorns bushes. These are the people who hear the word, but the worries of life, the deceitful pleasures of wealth, and the desires for other things come in and choke the word so that it can't produce a crop.

MARK 4:18–19 (ISV)

While working in my yard this summer, thanks to some raspberries and an ash tree, I learned again the insidious nature of what is left neglected.

You see, six years ago, we planted several raspberry plants along our back fence, along with a bed of strawberries, two cherry trees, and a few grapevines. As I bet you can tell, my family and I enjoy our homemade jams and jellies! That same year, the front yard got an Autumn Purple ash tree, surrounded by a bed of bulbs and perennials.

Fast-forward to last summer when the raspberries had really started taking over. New shoots cropped up everywhere, but they were manageable and mostly easy to ignore. They grew in the right places—mostly. But I noticed that they were getting uncomfortably close to the strawberries, cherries, and grapes. I meant to corral them, but I never quite got around to it.

This summer, however, I had to accept the consequences of my neglect. Instead of having gallons of fresh strawberries in early June, we harvested only one small bowl. The raspberries were choking them out and blocking the sunshine. Not only that, but the cherry trees had whole sections without blossoms because they were being surrounded. Oh, and did I mention that baby raspberry plants were even cropping up in the middle of the lawn?

What once was a small problem had become a major chore. It required many hours of work to solve it, and so much digging.

The lesson I learned? Pay attention to the little things, and don't ignore or neglect problems or annoyances. Take care of them *early*. And be aware of what's going on under the surface—roots can spread with destructive consequences.

And that lesson wasn't just about gardening. I asked God to point out areas of my life that I'm neglecting and to give me insight into what needs to be pruned.

God, help me live my life so that I can bear abundant fruit for You. Amen.

Summer Heat

CATHY BRYANT

But now, once at the end of the ages, He has appeared to put away sin by the sacrifice of Himself.

HEBREWS 9:26 (NKJV)

It was a hot August day when I traipsed out to my garden to check the rosebushes. Between hundred-degree heat and black spot disease, they weren't well. Most of their leaves were gone, and their thorny canes looked like thirsty hands stretched toward the sky, pleading for deliverance.

Though I had no control over the soaring temperatures, I had to take at least partial responsibility for the roses' demise. When I purchased the bushes, I'd been offered the opportunity to buy a fertilizer to help protect the plant from black spot. Interestingly enough, the product was called "Once." I remember that trivial detail because it struck me as odd that it had to be applied every six weeks instead of once, as the name suggested.

Had I not been so eager to save money and been more diligent about providing what the plants needed, my rosebushes would most likely have fared much better.

As a plant lovingly tended by the Gardener of my soul, I, too, have the tendency toward the black spot of sin. In addition, the scorching heat of the pressures and temptations of the world often leaves me pleading for more of my Living Water and His deliverance.

But there is great news! As our Creator and the one who tends the gardens of our lives, God knows *exactly* what we need. Through His Son Jesus, He has done all that is necessary to wipe away that black spot once and for all and refresh us with His Spirit.

By all these lovely tokens September days
are here, With summer's best of weather
And the autumn's best of cheer.

HELEN HUNT JACKSON

Just before the death of flowers, before they are buried in snow, there is a festival season when nature is aglow.

UNKNOWN

Fall

Take Heart

SHARON HINCK

Now finish the work, so that your eager willingness to do it may be matched by your completion of it, according to your means.

2 CORINTHIANS 8:11 (NIV)

I'm a great "starter." I instigate enthusiastic ideas, whether they involve cleaning a closet, canning jam, or planting a huge garden. However, I often get in over my head. Once all the items are pulled from the closet, the mess and disarray overwhelm me. After I get my canning supplies assembled, the many steps involved become daunting. And that huge garden? By early fall, the weeds win the battle as I tire of the project.

Follow through is also difficult as a disciple of Jesus. Like James and John, I might boldly leave everything to follow Him, then end up squabbling about who is the greatest in His eyes. Like Thomas, I may walk faithfully alongside the Savior, but then doubt His presence. Like Peter, I enthusiastically proclaim my loyalty to my Savior. Yet when confronted with social pressure, I shrink into myself, unable to even admit I know Him.

Sometimes we think life should get easier as time goes by, but it's often during the last stretch of the race when a runner's muscles scream to quit. The last contractions of childbirth are the fiercest.

Are you in a place of exhaustion, feeling unable to finish the work of serving Jesus where He has placed you today? Take heart! Even as He calls us to endure, He also promises to work in and through us.

~ Don't Compare ~

This year's garden doesn't compare itself to last year's garden nor to the one next door. A willow tree doesn't strain to get a glimpse of the oak down the road. An eagle soaring up above a mountain lake doesn't busy himself by measuring his wingspan against that of the red-tailed hawk below him.

God has created endless variety and diversity in the natural world. We are wise to refrain from comparison—either with others or with the past—and instead look with hope and gratitude toward the future, trusting in God's promises.

Roses and Thorns

CATHY BRYANT

"Be kind and compassionate to one another, forgiving each other, just as in Christ God forgave you."

EPHESIANS 4:32 (NIV)

Do you know the comic strip *Ziggy*? Published since the 1960s, Ziggy is a bald character with few defining features. People love him because Ziggy deals with relatable misfortunes, ones we all have to handle. In one strip, for instance, he says, "You can complain because roses have thorns, or rejoice because thorns have roses."

Let's take a brief look at roses. You already know that roses have sharp spikes or thorns. But did you know that botanists call them "prickles"? They believe that roses have thorns to protect themselves from being eaten by animals, who smell their beautiful fragrance and might want to eat them for dinner. Rose thorns often point downward, preventing critters from climbing up the stem and chomping on the gorgeous blooms.

Most of us have been pierced by a rose thorn at one time or another, but others have had more serious interactions after being scratched or pricked. Rose-thorn disease is a fungus that can be found on the tips of rose thorns. When a person is affected by this fungus, infection can spread throughout the body and even attack the central nervous system. By wearing garden gloves when handling roses, a person can prevent real harm.

You might be wondering what this has to do with our spiritual lives. Well, sometimes we get scratched or pricked by something sharp: another person's unkind words, a hard situation, or even disappointment with ourselves. That tiny puncture wound might heal in a day or two, or it could cause further, more systemic problems in our minds and hearts. This might come in the form of bitterness or grudges or other forms of unforgiveness.

Other than prayer, the best way I know of releasing the thorns and spiritual infection is to remember this: God will never ask us to forgive others any more than what He's already forgiven us.

So let's leave the thorns and their complaints behind and reach for the rose instead.

Let us not forget that the cultivation of the earth is the most important labor of man. When tillage begins, other arts will follow. The farmers, therefore, are the founders of civilization.

DANIEL WEBSTER

Hope and Grace

JEANETTE LEVELLIE

In all my prayers for all of you, I always pray with joy.

PHILIPPIANS 1:4 (NIV)

Sadly, I can no longer work in the garden like I used to, but I've imagined new ways to enjoy my plants and the beloved outdoors. Now I plant petunias, coleus, and zinnias in huge, colorful pots.

With the help of my granddaughter, a flower bed that had been overrun every spring with Goliath-sized crabgrass has been transformed into a maintenance-free rock garden. We've adorned it with large stones that are engraved with the words "Hope" and "Grace." River rocks, nestled between these stones, complete the lovely, peaceful scene.

Caring for the potted plants and maintaining the rock garden takes more time than I had expected, but my God-given gift of imagination will not let me surrender. Whenever I close my eyes, I can see the finished work of art, the garden that reminds me of the hope and grace God promises to those who love Him.

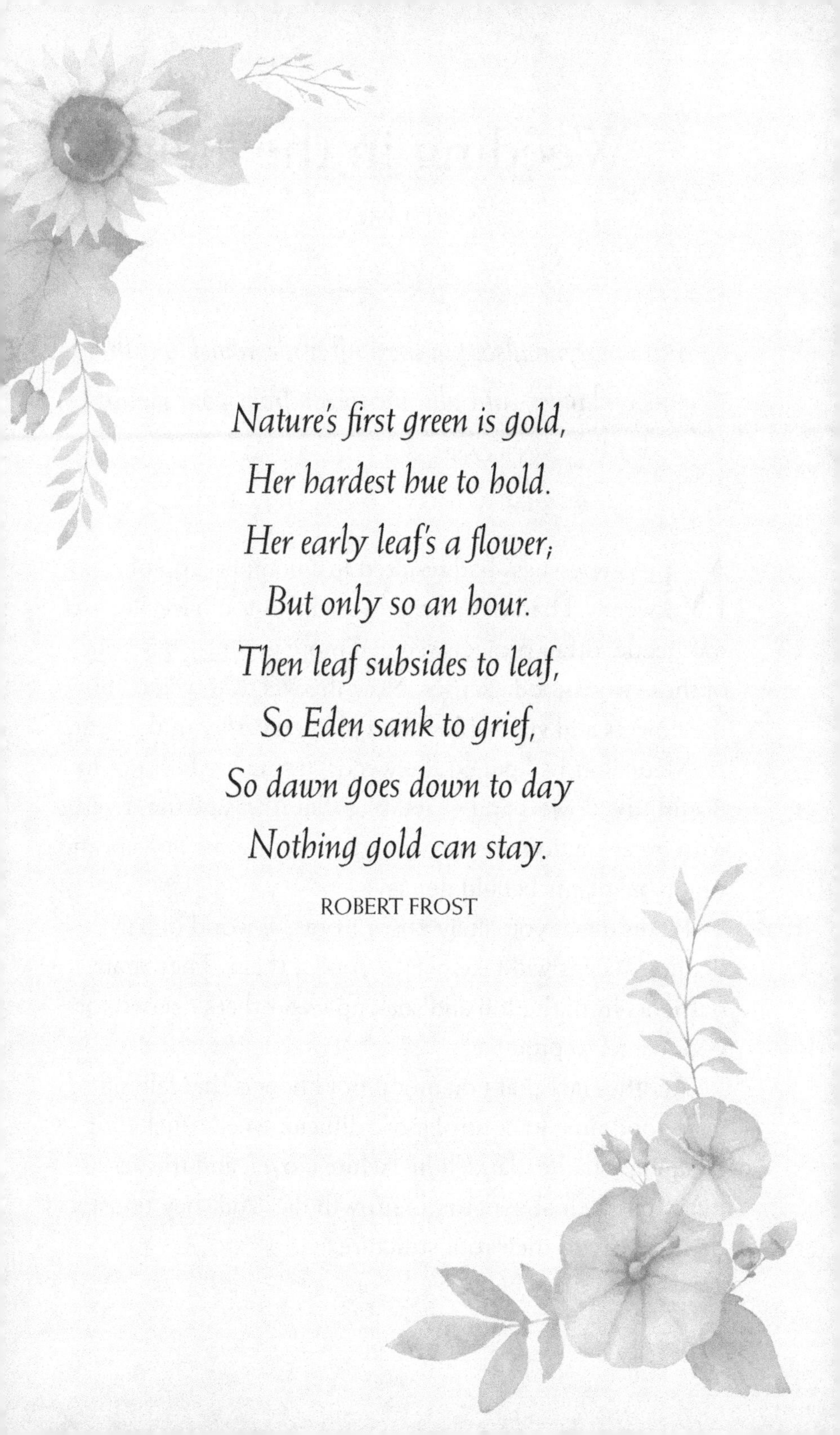

Nature's first green is gold,
Her hardest hue to hold.
Her early leaf's a flower;
But only so an hour.
Then leaf subsides to leaf,
So Eden sank to grief,
So dawn goes down to day
Nothing gold can stay.

ROBERT FROST

Weeding in the Fall

CATHY BRYANT

But now you also, put them all aside: anger, wrath, malice, slander, and abusive speech from your mouth.

COLOSSIANS 3:8 (NASB1995)

My carelessness had resulted in a bumper crop of weeds. I had lots of excuses—I was too busy, life was too hectic, other projects seemed more urgent—but none of these were good excuses. Now the weeds towered above the flowers and vegetables I had planted earlier in the year.

Meticulously, I pulled the weeds, trying my best not to disturb the flowers and vegetables. But it was no use. Even with great caution on my part, there were some flowers and vegetable plants I could not save.

Here's a fact you likely know from the world of gardening: Weeds will take over if you let them. They drain nutrients from the soil and soak up water that's needed for your plants to produce.

Another fact that you might not know is that fall is a very good time to control more difficult weeds, including creeping Charlie, dandelions, white clover, and thistles. Every fall their aboveground growth dies and they transfer their energy to their root structure.

As I weed my garden beds this autumn, I think about what might be growing in the garden of my heart. What can I rid myself of as I prepare for winter? How can I gently pull out those weeds by the roots so they don't grow deeper into my life?

Ask your loving Gardener to show you what you need to pull in order to someday bear the good fruit He has for you to produce.

Lord God, show me what I need to pull out in order to someday bear the good fruit You want me to produce. Give me strength to nurture and sustain others and to let them know about Your love. Amen.

REFLECTIONS

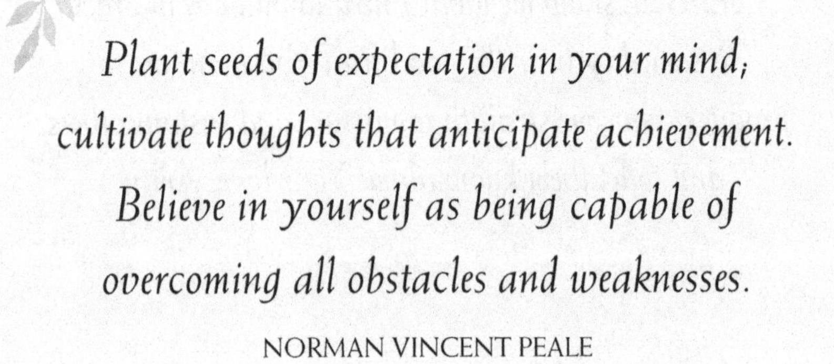

Plant seeds of expectation in your mind;
cultivate thoughts that anticipate achievement.
Believe in yourself as being capable of
overcoming all obstacles and weaknesses.

NORMAN VINCENT PEALE

Harvest Boon

VIRGINIA POEHLEIN

Freely you have received, freely give.

MATTHEW 10:8 (NIV)

The beans hung heavy on the vine. We also had a bumper crop of tomatoes—more than I could ever can. And my husband was so tired of zucchini casseroles that he wanted to plow the garden under.

"Let's give the surplus away," I said.

An old metal rack and a large bread tray formed my roadside stand. I loaded it up with okra, sweet potatoes, green beans, tomatoes, peas, radishes, and bell peppers from our garden. On a big sign I painted "Help Yourself," and provided bags, each containing a scripture verse written on a piece of paper.

Notes and gifts appeared, replacing the vegetables that had been taken. Fruit, Scripture bookmarks, a package of freshly dressed catfish, a lapel pin, even trading stamps were left behind. Some people called or came to our door to thank us.

Now I can hardly wait to gather vegetables in the morning. Some we keep for ourselves; the rest replenish our stand.

As the Gospel says, "Freely, ye have received, freely give."

Blackberry Time

JERI LYNN STOLTENBERG

And my God will meet all your needs according to the riches of his glory in Christ Jesus.

PHILIPPIANS 4:19 (NIV)

I carried my wooden stool to the blackberry patch behind my dad's garage. The October day was crisp, and I was glad I had bundled up. The berries would still be small, but I had to harvest them before the first frost. I dug into the ground and lifted out the first bush. Turning it upside down, I expected to see clusters of dark purple, but to my dismay all I saw were green clumps—not enough ripe berries to make the Russian-German delicacies we treasured.

The past year had been hard. Both my mom and grandma had died. I thought of how we used to work together as a family fixing blackberry dumplings, *gefüllte Klösse*. My mind drifted back to last year's harvest when Grandma, Mom, and I sat in the garage for hours, picking clumps of purple-black berries.

A brisk gust blew my scarf in my face and brought me back to the present. Tears started down my cheeks and I put my head in my hands. Like the unripe berries, I hadn't been prepared when I lost my mom and then my grandma. I certainly didn't feel ready to carry the responsibilities they had shouldered.

Maneuvering the small stool between the rows, I picked for two hours. When my fingers were too cold to continue, I had a mere two cups, not enough for anything. I went home all but empty-handed. I couldn't bear to tell my dad or my brothers. I cleaned and drained the few berries and put them in the freezer that evening. Then I crawled into bed, emotionally spent.

But the next morning the frost hadn't appeared. At the end of the week I returned to the patch and found that the berries had all ripened. In silence, I picked each bush. The longer I picked, the lighter my heart became.

In His good time, God had ripened the blackberries; in His time He would heal my grief. This was my season to mourn; peace would not be far away.

REFLECTIONS

A Weed Named Esau

SCOTT WALKER

Bless me, even me also, O my father!

GENESIS 27:34 (AMPC)

Last year, in the midst of blooming hibiscus, hanging ferns, and multiple forms of flowering plants, one of my ceramic pots remained fallow and empty. Borne by the wind, a tiny seed penetrated the soil and soon a tall, vigorous stalk was growing and vibrant green leaves sprouted.

When a neighbor visited, I pointed to the nomadic plant and asked, "Do you know what this is?"

"Yes, it's a weed!" she said, smiling. "It will take over a garden in a minute. You need to get rid of it."

The next day I picked up the potted weed and headed to the garbage can. But as I did, I felt a pang of sadness. This plant was truly beautiful, and because someone declared it "a weed," I was discarding it and ending its life.

I returned the weed to the porch, watered it, and decided to name my plant Esau, who was supposed to inherit his father Isaac's blessing and heritage until, in a moment of classic deception, his younger twin brother, Jacob, tricked his father and stole Esau's blessing. As a result, Esau was spurned by his family, cast away, and rejected without inheritance from the garden of rich Jewish history.

Today, as fall is upon us, Esau remains prominent in my front porch garden to remind me that in the kingdom of God, everyone receives a blessing, everyone has worth, and everyone can reflect the glory of God.

At no other time [than autumn] does the earth let itself be inhaled in one smell, the ripe earth; in a smell that is in no way inferior to the smell of the sea, bitter where it borders on taste, and more honeysweet where you feel it touching the first sounds. Containing depth within itself, darkness, something of the grave almost.

RAINER MARIA RILKE

Lesson from a Squirrel

CATHY BRYANT

See to it that no one falls short of the grace of God and that no bitter root grows up to cause trouble and defile many.

HEBREWS 12:15 (NIV)

Outside, a squirrel was hurriedly burying a pecan in my garden. I watched from a nearby window and heaved a sigh. That nut would become yet another tree for me to dig out of the flower beds next spring.

Watching this familiar scene, I reflected on the fact that, sadly, I have been like that squirrel, digging a hole in my heart and stuffing down strong emotions I didn't want to deal with at the time. I thought I was doing the right thing by hiding my hurt, but the results were even more catastrophic than the pecan saplings that appear each spring in my garden.

The anger and hurt I have refused to deal with have grown into saplings and even full-grown trees of bitterness and resentment. It's taken a lot of work to dig them out and clear the flowerbeds of my heart again. I've only been able to do this impossible work with God's help.

If you're like me and tend to bury the emotions you don't want to deal with—don't! I speak from experience: "Buried nuts" can take root, grow strong, and unleash a world of hurt on us and those around us.

Instead of squirrelling our pain away, we can call on the resources that are ours through God and His Word. The Bible gives us clear directives—including how to deal with our anger quickly, live at peace with others, and forgive as we've been forgiven.

Forgiveness is difficult work, but when we take the time to remember all that Christ has forgiven for us, it makes it easier. It helps to remember that carrying around the heavy weight of unforgiveness only hurts us.

I watched the squirrel until he ran up a tree at the back of my yard, grateful for God's reminder to deal honestly with my pain and not bury it away.

REFLECTIONS

A Thorny Lesson

GAIL THORELL SCHILLING

How much better to get wisdom than gold, to get insight rather than silver!

PROVERBS 16:16 (NIV)

A truckload of horse manure once taught me a valuable lesson in humility.

I had just moved from Boston to Lander, Wyoming, and couldn't wait to start my first vegetable garden. Yet here where cows and horses outnumber humans, I found stores selling twenty-pound bags of manure.

I asked my neighbor, a rancher and lifelong Wyomingite, why anyone would pay for manure when it could be had for free. He assured me store-bought treated fertilizer was better and began to explain. Ignoring the fact that he knew the land well and thinking myself smarter than him, I barely listened.

So when a friend who raised horses offered me all the manure I wanted, I loaded up a borrowed truck, hauled it home, and spread the manure on my garden—all twenty-five-by-forty feet of it. As I worked, I thought of my rancher neighbor and everyone else who was wasting their money on manure. I felt proud of the money I had saved, even smug. And, as the weather warmed, my vegetable seeds sprouted in tidy rows. But soon thistles, prickly thorny weeds, grew in crazy profusion around my plants, often smothering my seedlings.

I complained to my rancher friend about the infestation of stinging weeds.

"Yup, that can happen when stock grazes in the wrong pasture," he said. "I tried to warn you: Digestive juices don't harm the seeds a bit. I'm afraid you've got yourself some thistles."

For the next seventeen years, I wrestled thistles from my garden. Along the way, I learned that this weed with stinging spines could sprout vertical as well as lateral roots. If I yanked them straight up and out, the remaining root grew sideways. If I chopped them with a hoe, I just made more pieces, which grew into more plants. Interestingly, the locals who purchased the treated fertilizer didn't have my problem.

I now know that the composting process generates enough heat to kill unwanted seeds and bacteria. I now also know that I need to listen, with humility, to people who are wiser than I am.

Growing Up in God

CATHY BRYANT

Therefore, putting aside all malice and all deceit and hypocrisy and envy and all slander, like newborn babies, long for the pure milk of the word, so that by it you may grow in respect to salvation.

1 PETER 2:1–2 (NASB1995)

No plant begins its life in fruit production mode. Instead plants begin as tiny seedlings that must soak up moisture and nourishment from the soil in order to grow stronger and more resilient so that, one day, they may produce fruit.

Just as plants must mature, so must we as human beings. We can't stay babies forever; we need to mature both physically *and* spiritually to grow into the people God intended us to be.

In every garden, for the health of the plants that grow there, there are things that must be taken away—things like pests, rocks, and weeds. There are also things that must be added for the garden's health, such as water, nutrients, and adequate sunlight.

The same is true of our spiritual lives. To grow spiritually mature, there are some things, such as deceit, hypocrisy, and slander, that we need to root out of our lives. Instead we can take in the "pure milk" of God's nourishing Word in order to grow closer to Him.

Heavenly Father, none of us are born knowing everything. We learn to crawl before we walk, and at first our steps are shaky and slow. Then one day we learn to run. Lord, help us all to see the necessity of maturing in our faith. May we long to grow up in You so we can produce more and better fruit for You and Your Kingdom. Amen.

~ Accept Fallow Times ~

Farmers use a technique called "fallowing" to help land rest and regenerate. Fallowing simply means choosing not to sow seeds but letting soil remain idle for a season or two. While fallow, the land stores moisture and nutrients. Fallowing is done to maximize future harvests.

When your life feels quiet, unproductive, and even fruitless, consider in what ways God might be choosing to let you lie fallow, healing you and preparing you for future growth and harvests.

A Different Kind of Composting

CANDEE FICK

And we know that in all things God works for the good of those who love him, who have been called according to his purpose.

ROMANS 8:28 (NIV)

Part of preparing the soil of our garden includes adding organic material to the soil, and nothing beats the "black gold" of compost.

Compost, that mixture of decaying organic matter that is used as fertilizer. Where else can refuse like used coffee grounds, banana peels, shredded newspaper, and grass clippings be transformed into something of vital use? It's something that will nourish my plants, resulting in a more abundant harvest.

Creating quality compost doesn't happen overnight. It takes heat and time to transform the rotting material into the rich fertilizer that feeds the soil.

God does the same in my life. Given enough time, even my old mistakes and disappointments can be transformed into rich material that promotes growth in my life and nourishes the lives of those around me.

I'll give you an example. As a young teen and throughout high school, I was an extremely shy introvert. I felt the pain and loneliness of being a wallflower. The insecurity of not having close friends. The awkwardness of wanting to say something yet being too afraid of rejection to speak.

The bottom line is that those are years I'd rather forget. But when I walk into a room today and see someone hanging back, I reach out. I make sure to include the people who otherwise would hover in the corner, like I used to do. My social issues as a teen have taught me how to include people and to cultivate quality relationships.

Now that's compost at its finest.

Earth knows no desolation. She smells regeneration in the moist breath of decay.

GEORGE MEREDITH

Divine Abundance

GAIL THORELL SCHILLING

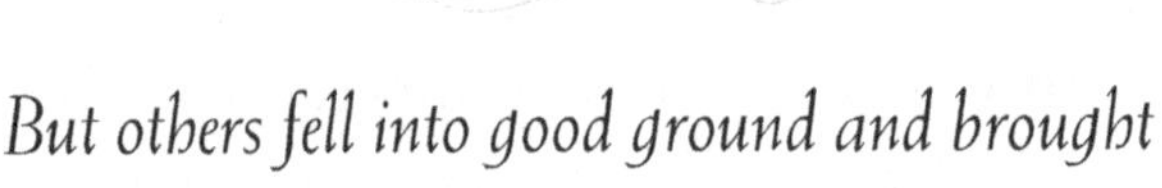

But others fell into good ground and brought forth fruit, some an hundredfold.

MATTHEW 13:8 (KJV)

In spring the first Chinooks come. Chinooks are warm, dry winds that signal the end of winter for us here on the east side of the Rocky Mountains. They raise temperatures thirty degrees in as many minutes, and we folks in Wyoming's Lander Valley turn our thoughts to gardening.

My own plot of rich, river-bottom soil produced well for my family. As a single mom, I depended upon these vegetables. Then, one particularly challenging year, when I worried incessantly about every last nickel, God used pumpkins to remind me that He always provides.

While shopping, I discovered seeds for ten cents a package, perfect for my strained budget. I scooped up seeds to grow tomatoes, green beans, zucchini, lettuce, radishes, onions, beets, peas, and pumpkins. I hadn't planted potatoes that year, so I had space for six generous hills of pumpkins, which would sprawl and consume the vacant space.

That year, frost held off, so by the end of September I had a bumper crop, a golden mound of pumpkins weighing five to ten pounds apiece. Even after the kids had chosen their jack-o'-lanterns and I had set aside a few for pies, I still had plenty of pumpkins.

As I shopped for potatoes the next day, I jokingly asked the produce manager if he needed pumpkins.

"Sure do!" he said. "I'll give you fifteen cents a pound."

About a week later, I received a check for fifteen dollars, a modest windfall but a tremendous return on a ten-cent investment. Once again, I knew that if I would plant and tend my garden, if I would be a good steward of what little I had, God would take care of the rest.

Through Jesus, therefore, let us continually offer to God a sacrifice of praise—the fruit of lips that openly profess his name.

HEBREWS 13:15 (NIV)

Sprouting New Growth

SHAWNELLE ELIASEN

And the God of all grace, who called you to his eternal glory in Christ, after you have suffered a little while, will himself restore you and make you strong, firm, and steadfast.

1 PETER 5:10 (NIV)

We were having a family workday, and all five of our sons were set loose on the lawn with rakes, shears, spades, and two wheelbarrows. Our son Logan offered to prune the bush out front. It was sprawling and out of shape, creating a hazard when we backed down the driveway.

"I'll Google pruning first," he said, "so I know just how to do it."

"Sold!" I said and handed him the electric clippers.

An hour later my husband, Lonny, poked his head through the kitchen door.

"Shawnelle," he called, "better come out."

I followed him and what I saw made my breath come fast.

"The bush!" I exclaimed. "It's ruined."

Logan stood at the end of the drive, saw buzzing and branches falling. The bush looked like a naked claw jutting out of the ground. Lush green branches pooled around his ankles. For the rest of the summer, each time I saw what remained of the bush, I winced and looked away.

But now it's fall. New growth is beginning to appear on the branches. It's evident that the bush will be stronger and healthier in the end.

As a family, we've had some tough times this year. Lonny and I have often felt stripped down, sheared, bare, and exposed.

After a long season, however, our family is healing. We're sprouting new growth.

In the end, like that pruned bush, we'll be stronger, lovelier, for it all.

REFLECTIONS

October Blooms

REBECCA BARLOW JORDAN

For I will pour out water to quench your thirst.

ISAIAH 44:3 (NLT)

When I was first designing the garden patches around my house, I decided to plant perennials as well as annuals—mostly ferns. These required watering by hand, and I got into a regular pattern of caring for them. My usual trek around the north, west, and east sides of the house included lugging a plastic container filled with water to quench their thirst. I rarely visited the sunny south side.

Months later, when I was walking in front of my home, I spotted a bit of gold along the south side of my house. *What could that be?* I detoured up my neighbor's driveway to take a closer look.

There, against the side of the house, nestled between hedges of holly bushes with their sharp, thorny leaves, sat beautiful, golden irises in full bloom—in October! I had first transplanted a bunch of those thirty-year-old irises from my mom's house almost two decades earlier. But in my shady backyard, they had not done well. In order for them to grow and flourish, I had transplanted them in one of the few sunny spots in our yard and then forgotten about them. What a surprise to see those flowers thriving!

Enjoying those irises meant adding an important ritual to my normal watering and walking patterns: checking out the sunny side. If I failed to do this, I'd miss a beautiful part of God's creation. Sure enough, those golden irises bloomed again in the spring.

Enjoying the sunny side of life begins with the Son Himself—this means spending time with Jesus. When we make moments with Him a part of our normal routine, rooted in His Word and with faith in our eyes, we'll see "gold." Jesus will quench our own thirst with His living water, and we'll experience new joys and surprises we previously neglected to notice.

Your land will be plowed again, and nobody will be able to see that it was once barren. Instead, they will say that it looks as beautiful as the garden of Eden. They won't see towns lying in ruins, but they will see your strong cities filled with people. Then the nearby nations that survive will know that I am the one who rebuilt the ruined places and replanted the barren fields. I, the LORD, make this promise.

EZEKIEL 36:34–36 (CEV)

A Blessing from Above

CATHY BRYANT

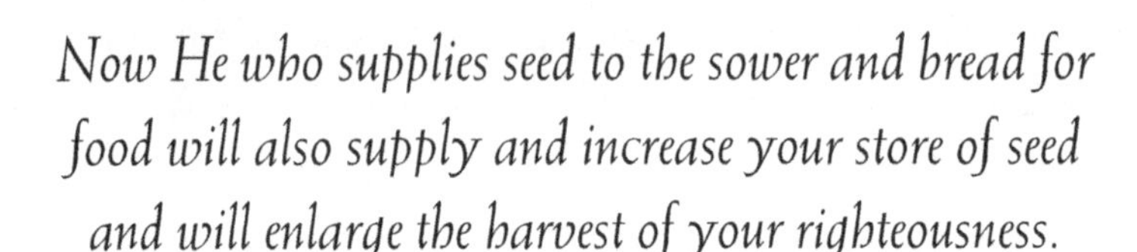

Now He who supplies seed to the sower and bread for food will also supply and increase your store of seed and will enlarge the harvest of your righteousness.

2 CORINTHIANS 9:10 (NIV)

The wonderful thing about bumper crops is that their harvests are well above and beyond what is planted, toiled for, or expected. Bumper crops can feel like miracles, and actually God blessed His people in the Bible by giving them abundant "bumper crop" harvests.

Recently I've experienced that very miracle in my wheat harvest, and it felt like a generous blessing from above!

You see, last year, I experimented with growing wheat for the first time. And right from the start, it grew beautifully! I was delighted. But then, just before I was planning to harvest it, a fierce hailstorm pummeled the field. Those ice pellets battered the stalks of wheat, knocking the grain right out of the florets.

I was devastated. After the storm, my beautiful wheat looked beaten down and pitiful. Though I went ahead and harvested what I could, the ground was dotted with individual grains that had fallen prematurely because of the hail.

Then a couple of weeks later, I noticed something surprising. Seedlings were poking their tiny green heads out of the ground where the previous wheat crop had been planted. On closer inspection, I realized that the hailstorm had been a blessing in disguise. I ended up harvesting much more wheat than I started with; it was truly a bumper crop!

Even when we are going through the normal storms of life, God can create new growth and even abundance for us. He will bless us, even through what seems like the remnants or broken parts of our lives.

Thank You, God, for the way You plant Your Word in our lives. Make us bold and fearless in sharing our faith and the bumper crop of Your love with others. Thank You for working through all things for those of us who love You. Amen.

FROM

"IL PENSEROSO"

BY JOHN MILTON

While the bee with honied thigh,
That her flowery work doth sing,
And the waters murmuring
And such consort as they keep,
Entice the dewy-feather'd sleep.

Flight of the Bumblebee

CANDEE FINK

"Jesus replied, 'What is impossible with man is possible with God.'"

LUKE 18:27 (NIV)

Have you ever watched bumblebees fly? Tiny wings carry their relatively large bodies from flower to flower.

People used to insist that bumblebees aren't supposed to be able to fly. That is, someone once did a few simple calculations and determined that it would be *impossible* for a bumblebee to remain airborne according to the laws of aerodynamics.

Tell that to the bumblebee!

Actually, though, a more sophisticated analysis showed that bumblebees can fly because their wings operate more like helicopter blades. So although they couldn't take flight like a bird or a plane, it makes sense that they can fly. Their muscles vibrate rather than expand and contract, allowing them to beat their wings ten to twenty times faster than if they relied on nerve firing impulses alone.

So, no, it's not impossible for bees to fly!

And maybe, like the bumblebee, you will defy what others see as reality! Everything is possible with God.

The Healing Garden

HELEN GRACE LESCHEID

The LORD will guide you always; he will satisfy your needs in a sun-scorched land and will strengthen your frame. You will be like a well-watered garden, like a spring whose waters never fail.

ISAIAH 58:11 (NIV)

Dave was doing his regular volunteer stint at the Salvation Army, where he taught guitar, when he noticed the ugly yard out back.

Before he began a twenty-five-year career as a teacher, Dave had been a landscaper. Seeing the empty lot, he had a thought: *That could be made into a beautiful garden where our clients could find some peace*. The idea caught fire. Residents and clients helped clear the land, nurseries donated plants, community organizations provided funds. It was named "The Healing Garden."

During the opening ceremony of the garden, I reveled in the beauty of the beds of purple, blue, and yellow flowers set against a green hillside with a miniature waterfall trickling nearby. Flowers bloomed from a pair of brown rubber boots and an old blue suitcase. Off to one side were garden plots in which clients grew beets, strawberries, tomatoes, and brussels sprouts to be used in the Salvation Army's kitchen.

A band of six men strummed guitars and banjos and sang "What a Friend We Have in Jesus" and "Amazing Grace." Then Dave picked up his guitar and sang a few of his own songs. The intensity with which they sang touched me.

"The men sing from personal experience," Dave explained. "As former addicts, they know what living on the streets is like."

"Were you singing from experience too?" I asked.

"I was never an addict," he said slowly, "but I've gone through a lot of other things in my life. I understand their pain."

Thank You, Father, for using our suffering to grow our love and empathy for others. Amen.

Oh, the comfort, the inexpressible comfort of feeling safe with a person; having neither to weigh thoughts nor measure words, but to pour them all out, just as they are, chaff and grain together, knowing that a faithful hand will take and sift them, keep what is worth keeping, and then, with a breath of kindness, blow the rest away.

DINAH MARIA MULOCK CRAIK

Connected to the Vine

KIRSTEN HOLMBERG

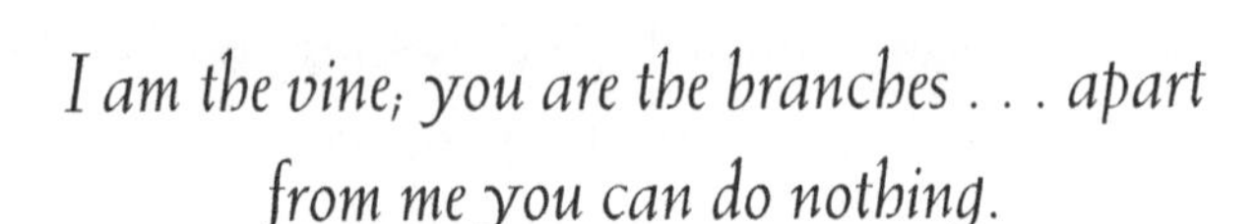

I am the vine; you are the branches . . . apart from me you can do nothing.

JOHN 15:5 (NIV)

I was excited to move to our new home across town but sad to leave behind my favorite plant, a beautiful and somewhat rare variety of clematis.

After unsuccessfully scouring the local nurseries for another one, I resorted to trimming off a few branches in hopes of transplanting them to my new yard. Despite my best efforts to root and plant them, the branches withered and died.

While a more skilled gardener might have succeeded, this frustrating experience reminded me of how I need to remain connected to Jesus, the Vine, who sustains and supports me, apart from whom I can do nothing.

Best of all, the Vine holds on to its branches—not the other way around—making me both secure and fruitful.

Jesus, thank You for being the Vine that secures and sustains me and brings forth fruit in my life. Amen.

"NEARER, MY GOD, TO THEE"

BY SARAH F. ADAMS

Nearer, my God, to Thee, nearer to Thee!
E'en though it be a cross that raiseth me,
Still all my song shall be, nearer, my God, to Thee.
Nearer, my God, to Thee, nearer to Thee!

Though like the wanderer, the sun gone down,
Darkness be over me, my rest a stone;
Yet in my dreams I'd be nearer, my God, to Thee.
Nearer, my God, to Thee, nearer to Thee!

There let the way appear, steps unto Heav'n;
All that Thou sendest me, in mercy giv'n;
Angels to beckon me nearer, my God, to Thee.
Nearer, my God, to Thee, nearer to Thee!

That old September feeling, left over from school days, of summer passing, vacation nearly done, obligations gathering, books and football in the air . . . Another fall, another turned page: there was something of jubilee in that annual autumnal beginning, as if last year's mistakes had been wiped clean by summer.

WALLACE STEGNER

Something Has to Die

CATHY BRYANT

Truly, truly, I say to you, unless a grain of wheat falls into the earth and dies, it remains alone; but if it dies, it bears much fruit.

JOHN 12:24 (ESV)

There is nothing like a garden to so aptly portray the life cycle. One of the ways it does so is through the practice of composting, a process by which leaves, grass clippings, and other plant matter decompose and create rich soil.

I'm always amazed at how dead and decaying plants can contain such life-nurturing organic compounds. Compost eventually acts as a fertilizer for living plants, restoring and energizing the soil to help them bring forth an abundant harvest.

What a glorious portrayal of what Christ has done for us! Because of His great love for us, He died, releasing us from the wages of our sin and overcoming death once and for all. Because of His death and resurrection, we are given new life!

Just as a seed of grain dies and drops to the earth, only to be reborn as stalks that will reproduce hundreds more, so we must die to ourselves and be reborn through Him, allowing our connection with Him to make us fruitful beyond our imagination.

Worth the Wait

MICHELLE MEDLOCK ADAMS

Wait for the Lord; be strong, and let your heart take courage; wait for the Lord!

PSALM 27:14 (ESV)

My sister, Martie, and I grew up in a home where we bought all our produce: Mama never had a garden. So, when my sister told me she had put out tomato plants last summer, I was quite impressed.

Because she was a novice gardener, Martie researched exactly how far apart to space her tomato plants, what kind of fertilizer to use, and how to keep destructive bugs away. Once the tomatoes were planted, she tended to them daily, anxiously awaiting the appearance of juicy fruit. But day after day, her plants didn't flower.

She couldn't figure it out. All of her neighbors who had also planted tomatoes were already enjoying the fruit of their labor. Martie kept wondering what she had done wrong.

Frustrated, Martie gave in and went to the Saturday morning farmer's market in our hometown in search of fresh tomatoes. While paying, Martie told the farmer her plight.

"I just don't get it," she said. "All of my neighbors who put out tomato plants the same time I did have tomatoes, but I still don't have any."

The farmer paused to think for a moment, and then he asked, "Well, what type of tomatoes did you plant?"

"You mean there are different kinds?" Martie asked.

He nodded, and began rattling off a list of various kinds of tomatoes. I've since learned that there are more than 10,000 types, from Adoration to Yellow Pear!

"I think they were called Big Boy," Martie said.

"Well there's your problem," the farmer explained. "Big Boy tomatoes have a ninety-five-day gestation period whereas other tomato plants can produce fruit in as little as seventy days...you just have to wait a little longer for the Big Boys, but they're my favorites."

Makes me wonder how many of us have "Big Boy" dreams in our hearts placed there by God, yet we just don't realize that they take longer to come to fruition. But when God brings them forth, they will be better than we could ever imagine. They're so worth the wait!

New Life

TEZ BROOKS

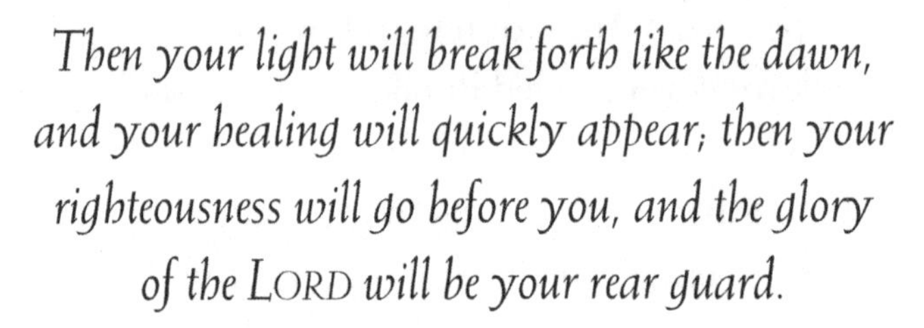

Then your light will break forth like the dawn, and your healing will quickly appear; then your righteousness will go before you, and the glory of the LORD will be your rear guard.

ISAIAH 58:8 (NIV)

Our new sapling thrived for a while, with flowers blooming in spring. But each year, the tree waned. Its leaves became sparse, and it stopped blooming. Years of sitting in the wrong spot took its toll. The tree turned into an ugly stick in the ground.

That fall, after bending one of the branches, it snapped off in my hand. Sadly, I was about to give up—until my fingernail scraped a small amount of bark from the trunk, exposing a moist green center filled with life.

I gently dug up the root ball and relocated the stick next to a sprinkler. Today, that tree is taller than me, blanketed in lush foliage.

When I neglect God's Word, I'm like that tree—slowly losing ground, producing little to indicate growth. I can appear dead and hopeless.

Thankfully, God never gives up; He gently leads me back to His Word and takes gentle steps to revive me.

FROM

"LET ALL CREATION BLESS THE LORD"

BY CARL P. DAW

Let all creation bless the Lord,
till heaven with praise is ringing.
Sun, moon, and stars, peal out a chord,
stir up the angels' singing.
Sing, wind and rain! Sing, snow and sleet!
Make music, day, night, cold, and heat:
exalt the God who made you.

All living things upon this earth,
green fertile hills and mountains,
sing to the God who gave you birth;
be joyful, springs and fountains.
Lithe waterlife, bright airborne birds,
wild roving beasts, tame flocks and herds:
exalt the God who made you.

Transformation

CANDEE FINK

Do not conform to the pattern of this world, but be transformed by the renewing of your mind. Then you will be able to test and approve what God's will is—his good, pleasing and perfect will.

ROMANS 12:2 (NIV)

Life changes us—sometimes through heat, pressure, irritation, or being broken. But other times, we go through long, quiet periods. We find ourselves waiting in the dark for something to happen.

That makes me think about the butterflies I see in my garden.

This insect starts out as a worm, although we give it a fancier name: caterpillar. It spends its days crawling around and eating. As it grows, it sheds its old skin for new ones. Often caterpillars molt five times! While it might have interesting stripes and fuzzy hair, the caterpillar is anchored to the ground by gravity. Just like we are.

Then, one day, the caterpillar spins a cocoon and literally disappears—for a long time. Depending on what kind of caterpillar it is, it can be in the cocoon for five to twenty-one days! While inside, the caterpillar's tissue is broken down and a new structure is formed. This is the transformation stage.

At last, the cocoon shell is broken open and a butterfly emerges. Fragile, colorful wings are unfurled, and they test out the breeze. At last, the insect takes flight. No longer subject to gravity, it will take flight for the rest of its life, soaring and migrating to places it never imagined as a caterpillar.

So, how does this relate to you and me? Some days I feel like a worm, anchored down by my responsibilities. I move through life, ever trying to meet my own needs.

But then, a time of transformation comes. This often happens in the dark because I can't see what God is doing. Yet, I'm being changed from the inside out. While waiting in my cocoon, I feel cramped and uncomfortable. I can't wait to get out!

Finally, however, I feel myself breaking free. I see the light. I spread wings I didn't know I had. I gain altitude and a new perspective. I go places I could not have even dreamed of.

I am transformed.

REFLECTIONS

Transplanted to God's Garden

CATHY BRYANT

But we all, with unveiled face, beholding as in a mirror the glory of the Lord, are being transformed into the same image from glory to glory, just as by the Spirit of the Lord.

2 CORINTHIANS 3:18 (NKJV)

As the wife of a minister, I've moved a lot during my thirty-five-year marriage. There is something exciting and hopeful about starting over in a new place. In the depths of my heart, though, every single time we move there are parts of me that pray that *this* will be the last time.

Being transplanted isn't easy for most of us. It means ripping roots out of the ground and leaving the familiar for the unknown. My Texas yellow rose roots have had to adapt to new soils and new situations more times than I care to remember.

But, in retrospect, I can look back and see how God has used each and every stop of this earthly journey to grow me spiritually and to grow my character.

From the moment of my conversion from the old life to the new, I am transplanted from the world's garden into God's. And quite frankly, it can be difficult.

In the world's garden, I could grow—or not—according to my own plans and purposes. From my perspective in *that* garden, the options seem limitless. But whatever growth pattern I could choose in the world would leave me feeling empty and wondering: *Is this all there is?*

Once in God's garden, I had hoped that things would be completely trouble-free, that the Gardener would prevent me from encountering difficulty. But I quickly learned that the opposite is true. God allows me to go through heavy rains and storms. He constantly prods the soil around my roots in an attempt to loosen it so my roots can spread. He even prunes parts of me that I wasn't quite ready to let go.

But when I yield to His tending, within a few years I begin to sense a change. I see a result I never expected. Only then am I able to see that cooperating with God in the transplanting process was the best choice I ever made.

REFLECTIONS

Pulling Weeds

JULIA ATTAWAY

He must become greater; I must become less.

JOHN 3:30 (NIV)

On a recent Saturday morning, I went to the historic house up the street to do some weeding. I find weeding therapeutic—after doing the hard work you get to enjoy immediate gratification of a tidied space.

The Dyckman Farmhouse is incongruous amid the apartment buildings of northern Manhattan. It lies on Broadway across from a gas station, a sports bar, and a liquor store. The fact that this artifact of history exists is a minor miracle.

I'd been waging quiet war against weeds there for a while, but what bothered me most was the state of the street-front garden. Besides the challenges of overgrown bushes and the presence of invasive porcelain-berry, in the past I've felt intimidated about weeding the garden because it's a place where people experiencing homelessness live. Knowing I'd need to engage with strangers made me feel reticent.

But I finally faced my fears and decided to go for it.

And honestly, it was by far the best day of gardening I've had. As I clipped strands of out-of-control purple sage, I met two men who keep a broom hidden nearby to sweep up trash. Snipping ivy from a bench, a man and I joked together, and he helped me. I spoke with a woman who asked me for some of the clippings. She said she could make them into bouquets, sell them for a few dollars, and then have enough money to buy dinner that night. As I weeded, I watched her create beauty from the piles of cut leaves and vines. I had no reason to fear these folks.

At the end of the day, I hauled five huge armfuls of weeds to the compost pile. But best of all, I met a host of people I might have overlooked or even feared.

Now when I tackle the other half of the stretch of garden facing Broadway, I will do so as a neighbor and friend. After all, the only way to act like Christ to others is to encounter them. And sometimes pulling weeds together is the perfect way to connect.

A man of words and not of deeds,
Is like a garden full of weeds.

BENJAMIN FRANKLIN

Mr. Dowda's Grapevines

MIRIAM LONG

I know every bird of the mountains, and everything that moves in the field is Mine.

PSALM 50:11 (NASB)

In 1937, when I was ten years old, my family lived on the outskirts of Birmingham, Alabama. Mama had her hands full keeping my four brothers and me fed and clothed. But I had other concerns. I was tormented by curiosity about the man who lived in the dilapidated shack across the street. People told me to steer clear of him, that he'd turned his back on everybody, even God.

How can he live without God? I wondered. I decided to find out.

"Hi, mister," I announced one day. "I live across the street."

"Name's Dowda," he said.

Every day, I'd find an excuse to talk to him.

Once, Mr. Dowda was breaking up a small plot with a garden fork.

"What are you planting?" I asked.

"Grapevines," he said. "Watch if you want."

Sometimes I talked about Mr. Dowda at dinner, telling my family what I had learned. His wife and two sons had died in tragic accidents, and he had once worked in the construction business.

"No one ever visits that poor soul," Mama noted. From then on, she made a plate for him when she made our supper. I happily took the food over so I could learn more. I noticed then that Mr. Dowda did not bow his head or move his lips before taking his first forkful.

I grew to love him, but my concern about his faith persisted. I recited Bible verses I'd learned in Sunday school. He listened and nodded approvingly. But he never said anything about God.

When the grapes were ready for harvest, I helped Mr. Dowda pick the first bunch for Mama.

"Can't you do something to keep all these birds from getting so many?" I asked.

"Don't worry, girl. I made sure to plant enough for them too," he said. "Always do."

I remembered Jesus's words in the Bible about God caring for the birds. I realized that Mr. Dowda was helping Him. He *did* love God, and he showed it by sharing what little he had—and tolerating the outrageous curiosity of a young girl.

Harvesting the Garden of Life

CANDEE FICK

Let us not become weary in doing good, for at the proper time we will reap a harvest if we do not give up.

GALATIANS 6:9 (NIV)

After months of preparing, planting, watering, weeding, thinning, and waiting, the first vegetables were finally ready to pick. Baskets and bowls of sugar snap peas, radishes, carrots, and lettuce were transformed into salads. We had fresh corn on the cob and yellow summer squash. Cucumbers prepped in vinegar water and stuffed zucchini boats. And amazing salsa, made from tomatoes, onions, garlic, jalapeños, and cilantro. Later in the season, we'll have pumpkins to carve, and we'll roast the seeds.

Harvesting. Washing. Eating. Enjoying. Canning. Freezing. Sharing—especially that extra zucchini. It's the culmination of months of hard work and makes all the effort deliciously worth it.

This year, I've stirred up the rocky places of my life and let God turn my failures into rich compost. I've found good seeds to plant and been diligent to protect, weed, and thin the growth. I've done what I can do; the rest is up to God.

While I have waited, He's caused the seeds to grow into healthy plants, capable of bearing a plentiful harvest.

I ask myself: *What's growing in the garden of my life?* Faith. A solid marriage. The mentoring and care of my three children. Growing financial stability. Book ideas coming into fruition. I can hardly wait to see the full, bounteous harvest.

Dear God, I see the abundance in my harvest and again remember how You care for me and all of Your children—with a love and big-heartedness that never ceases to surprise and amaze me. Thank You for Your generosity. Amen.

REFLECTIONS

The Good Soil

KERI WYATT KENT

And the seed that fell on good soil represents those who hear and accept God's word and produce a harvest of thirty, sixty, or even a hundred times as much as had been planted!

MARK 4:20 (NLT)

So often, discussion of Jesus's parable of the seeds—as they fall on the path, onto rocky soil, into thorns, or onto good soil—focuses on the *harvest*. This verse is rightfully linked with Jesus's words in John 4:35, which says the fields are "ripe for harvest."

In the church I grew up attending, this harvest, ripe for the picking, has to do with winning converts to the faith. Since the parable comes after Jesus's conversation with the Samaritan woman and the subsequent conversion of many in her town, that makes sense. But so often we think, *What do I have to do to get busy harvesting?*

Yet Jesus is not comparing the good seed to a *farmer* who is doing the harvesting. Instead, He is saying that what makes the seed successful is the *soil* it falls onto—the right soil, the good soil.

Let's think about how soil becomes "good."

As a gardener, I can tell you that the soil can't become good on its own. In fact, the gardener has to work with it. It has to be broken apart so that is softened. It has to have rocks and weeds pulled from it. Good soil has organic matter in it: nutrients produced by the decay of dead leaves or by compost or manure. Circumstances in my life that, at the time, felt like "manure" have often been used by God to make the soil of my spiritual life more nutrient-rich and help me to grow. Into that good soil, God's Word takes root.

So if Jesus is telling us to be "good soil" so that our hearts can be fertile ground for His Word, we will need to submit to Him, allowing Him to break us, to pull the weeds of materialism and worry out from our hearts, and even "fertilize" us with experiences that cause us to become better people.

From this "good soil," we can then share the good news of God's love with others and help to make the harvest more abundant.

Hidden Rose

HEIDI GAUL

Though the LORD is exalted, he looks kindly on the lowly; though lofty, he sees them from afar.

PSALM 138:6 (NIV)

I adore flowers, and my husband, David, enjoys working the soil, so every year our yard comes alive with blossoms. From crocuses to irises to roses, you can almost tell what month it is by what is blooming. Maintaining our garden requires regular attention, and I spend a lot of time watering as David trims, plants, and weeds.

One day, as I lowered the hose into the well, I noticed a blotch of color near the dirt. Pulling the hose aside, I knelt beside a rosebush. There, just two inches above the ground, a delicate bud waited, sprouting from the base of an older branch.

Growing at a ninety-degree angle, its petals almost touched the dirt. Though ordinary in its appearance, it was an unexpected and welcome surprise. This hidden rose touched my heart more than all the flowers adorning the bush's crown.

It reminded me of my relationship with Christ. Even before I knew Him, Jesus saw me growing. He saw the potential for beauty in me. I might feel unworthy of Jesus's notice, but He saw me and found me. He *still* sees me and finds me today.

I asked my husband to snip the bud free. I put it in a vase and set it on our kitchen island where I could admire its singular beauty.

Whenever I entered that room and saw that rose, I thought of how Jesus saw me from afar and pulled me from my struggles into His unwarranted grace. He valued my soul's worth and put me in a place of honor.

REFLECTIONS

Fall Harvest

CATHY BRYANT

For even when we were with you, we commanded you this: If anyone will not work, neither shall he eat. For we hear that there are some who walk among you in a disorderly manner, not working at all, but are busybodies.

2 THESSALONIANS 3:10–11 (NKJV)

Make no mistake about it: For all its joys, gardening requires hard work. The effort it takes to weed, water, and otherwise care for a garden can tire us out. We might be tempted to give up before the harvest.

And, as is true in the garden or a farmer's field, getting to a place of *spiritual* harvest requires solid planning, careful maintenance, and hard work. Additionally, like a gardener, we reap exactly what we sow spiritually. We can't expect to plant beans to later harvest a crop of carrots. Nor can we expect to focus our energies only on material things and receive a spiritual harvest of God's peace, wisdom, and joy.

I find the best way to avoid discouragement and the desire to quit when I am working toward a spiritual harvest is to strengthen myself in the Lord. Through His Word and through prayer, God gives me what I need so that I will persevere. Though I might not ever experience the results

I hope for on this side of heaven, God promises that my efforts matter. And I'm promised my reward in heaven.

Oh, God, I confess that I often grow weary in my work for You, and I am sometimes tempted to give up. Lord, at those times, come to my rescue, comfort me, draw me close, and give me the strength I need to persevere. Thank You for the promise that I will reap an abundant harvest as I continue to do good. Amen.

The lesson I have thoroughly learnt, and wish to pass on to others, is to know the enduring happiness that the love of a garden gives.

GERTRUDE JEKYLL

Lessons from My Garden

MARY ANN O'ROARK

For this reason I kneel before the Father, from whom every family in heaven and on earth derives its name. I pray that out of his glorious riches he may strengthen you with power through his Spirit in your inner being, so that Christ may dwell in your hearts through faith. And I pray that you, being rooted and established in love, may have power, together with all the Lord's holy people, to grasp how wide and long and high and deep is the love of Christ.

EPHESIANS 3:14–19 (NIV)

In my earliest memories, I'm in my grandmother's yard in Ohio, reaching out to touch the soft petals of flowering phlox in lavender, rose, and snowy white. She holds my hand as we walk along what we called "hollyhock alley." Together, we sing a favorite hymn: "I come to the garden alone while the dew is still on the roses. . ."

Everything around me—the rustling leaves, the loamy scent of newly turned earth, the warmth of my grandmother's attention—assures me that this is a sacred place.

Is it any wonder that, all my life, I've made gardens for myself wherever I have lived?

My first apartment was a second-floor Manhattan walkup that looked out onto an air shaft. No light, no soil. I bought an aluminum stand with fluorescent lights to grow marigolds and geraniums.

My next place, and current home, is an apartment with a terrace and river view. I could have a garden here. Only problem: The place is seventeen blustery floors up. I hired a carpenter to build sturdy planters, and I picked up flats of impatiens and zinnias at street fairs. And I ordered hardy rosebushes to withstand the city's whipping winds.

I have to kneel on a narrow swath of brick to work my hands in the soil, but when I do, I feel as I did when I was a child. No matter where your garden grows, it enriches your life.

I've learned so much from gardens over the course of my life, but one of the best lessons has been to develop a strong root system.

I saw that on a gardening flyer, years ago. "DEVELOP A STRONG ROOT SYSTEM," it read in bold capital letters. *That's what a garden does for you*, I thought.

It keeps you rooted in your values, rituals, and traditions. It *roots* you.

A Note from the Editors

We hope you enjoyed *Finding God in the Garden,* published by Guideposts. For over 75 years, Guideposts, a nonprofit organization, has been driven by a vision of a world filled with hope. We aspire to be the voice of a trusted friend, a friend who makes you feel more hopeful and connected.

By making a purchase from Guideposts, you join our community in touching millions of lives, inspiring them to believe that all things are possible through faith, hope, and prayer. Your continued support allows us to provide uplifting resources to those in need. Whether through our communities, websites, apps, or publications, we inspire our audiences, bring them together, and comfort, uplift, entertain, and guide them.

To learn more, please go to guideposts.org.

We would love to hear from you:

To make a purchase or view our many publications, please go to shopguideposts.org
To call us, please dial (800) 932-2145
Or write us at Guideposts, P.O. Box 5815, Harlan, Iowa 51593

Made in the USA
Coppell, TX
20 April 2024